KiDS'
Bible
Facts

Kids' Bible Facts

ED STRAUSS

BARBOUR
PUBLISHING

Scripture quotations marked kjv are taken from the King James Version of the Bible.

Scripture quotations marked niv are taken from the Holy Bible, New International Version®. niv®. Copyright © 1973, 1978, 1984 by International Bible Society. Used by permission of Zondervan. All rights reserved.

Scripture quotations marked nkjv are taken from the New King James Version®. Copyright © 1982 by Thomas Nelson, Inc. Used by permission. All rights reserved.

Scripture quotations marked rsv are from the Revised Standard Version of the Bible, copyright 1946, 1952, 1971 by the Division of Christian Education of the National Council of the Churches of Christ in the USA. Used by permission.

Published by Barbour Publishing, Inc., P.O. Box 719, Uhrichsville, Ohio 44683 www.barbourbooks.com

Our mission is to publish and distribute inspirational products offering exceptional value and biblical encouragement to the masses.

Printed in the United States of America.

RR Donnelley, Willard, OH 44890; February 2010; D10002188

INTRODUCTION

Welcome to *Kids' Bible Facts*, a book of Bible information of all kinds. These pages are full of facts about familiar people, places, and things, but they're also stuffed with little-known and sometimes surprising details. (Did you know, for example, that all the gold in God's temple was looted *eight* times? Or that one king of Judah had 28 sons and 60 daughters?)

What's in this book specifically?

- *Who's That?*—short biographies of the greatest men and women, heroes and villains in the Bible, everyone from Eve to Felix, from Barak to Balak.
- *Peoples & Places*—details on people groups like the Ammonites, Canaanites, Edomites, Hittites—all the "ites"—and the far-flung, mysterious lands that these people lived in long ago.
- *And That Means. . .*—definitions of unusual Bible words like *atonement, impute*, and *covenant.* Once you've read these, you'll find it a whole lot easier to understand the Bible.
- *Features*—short accounts of well-known Bible characters doing amazing things you never heard about, as well as some crazy unknowns doing insane stuff that you just *know* they're not going to get away with!
- *I Love Lists!*—with titles like: "Eight People Who Came Back from the Dead," "Four Dusty, Desert Donkey Details," "10 Times That People Lived in Caves," and much, much more!
- *Fun Facts*—interesting and downright zany information, like how King Solomon had a round table 2,000 years before King Arthur, or how one father named his sons Huppim and Muppim. (If either of those happens to be your name, we're laughing *with* you, not *at* you!)

You'll notice throughout *Kids' Bible Facts* that each type of entry is color-coded—by looking at a headline, you can tell at a glance whether the entry is a biography, a definition, a "fun fact" or whatever. And when you see a colored word within the text, that means there's related information somewhere on the two-page "spread" you're looking at. Be sure to read the related items for the best understanding.

This handy little fact-finder will help you learn quickly what's what and who's who in the Bible. We trust you'll find it such fascinating reading that you'll come back to it again and again—and learn what's in your own Bible better and better.

AARON

Moses' older brother. God used Aaron and Moses to bring plagues on Egypt to try to convince Pharaoh to free the Israelites. Aaron later became high priest of Israel. (See: Exodus 7:1–7; 28:1–2.)

ABEDNEGO

King Nebuchadnezzar threw Shadrach, Meshach, and Abednego into a furnace for refusing to worship his idol, but God protected them. The king then made them officials of Babylon. (See: Daniel 3.)

King Nebuchadnezzar threw three men into the fiery furnace, but sees *four* in the flames—one looking "like the Son of God" (Daniel 3:24 KJV)

STRANGE BUT TRUE!
The Babylonians had bizarre ways of making decisions and getting directions. They killed a sheep, cut out its liver, and studied its markings and color for "messages." (See: Ezekiel 21:21.)

Four Powerful Priests Who Took Bold Action

1. Aaron ran in and saved the Israelites from a plague.
2. Phinehas speared an idolater and stopped a plague.
3. Jehoiada took over the government from the evil queen Athaliah.
4. Zechariah, son of Jehoiada, rebuked King Joash.

(See: Numbers 16:46–50; 25:1–11; 2 Kings 11:1–19; 2 Chronicles 24:17–23.)

I Love Lists!

WORSHIP

The Hebrew word for *worship* means "to bow down before someone" to show how much you honor them. We also worship God by praying, praising Him, by speaking about how great He is, or about the wonderful things that He has done. Worship also can be singing songs of praise to God. (See: Psalm 95:6; 145:1–12; 147:1.)

EGYPT (EGYPTIANS)

Egypt is a dry land in Africa, but the Nile River valley was very fertile. The Israelites lived there 430 years; Jesus was there when He was a child. (See: Exodus 12:40–41; Deuteronomy 11:10; Matthew 2:13–15.)

Places & People

Who's that?

ABEL

The first son of Adam and Eve. Abel, a shepherd, pleased God by sacrificing a lamb to Him. This caused his brother Cain to kill him in a fit of jealousy. (See: Genesis 4:1–15.)

ABIATHAR

The only priest to survive a massacre, Abiathar fled into the wilderness to join David as a fugitive. He later became a high priest of Israel. (See: 1 Samuel 22; 1 Chronicles 15:11.)

ABIGAIL

The wise wife of foolish Nabal. Abigail's quick thinking and generosity saved her whole household. After Nabal died of a heart attack, she married David. (See: 1 Samuel 25.)

THE NAME GAME!
The Israelites had only a *first* name and no middle name, so while there were guys named "Buz" (Genesis 22:21) and guys named "Bunni" (Nehemiah 11:15), you never hear of a "Buz Bunni."

THE NAME GAME!
What's in a name? One foolish Bible villain was named *Nabal*, meaning "fool." A New Testament Christian was named *Philologus*, meaning "lover of words." (See: 1 Samuel 25:25; Romans 16:15.)

And that Definition Means...

CONCUBINE

In ancient days, some men had more than one wife. Others chose to simply take a *concubine*—a slave who didn't have rights like a wife, but who slept with him and bore him children. If a man wished to get rid of his concubine, he gave her gifts, set her free, and sent her away. Abraham did this with his two concubines: Hagar and Keturah. (See: Genesis 16:1–4; 21:9–14; 25:5–6; 1 Chronicles 1:32.)

SACRIFICE

To give up something that is dear to you, or that costs you something. In the Law of Moses, the sacrifice God asked for was an animal—usually a lamb or a goat from the flock. In fact, *zebach*, which is the Hebrew word for *sacrifice*, means "a slaughtered animal." Paul said that Jesus was our Passover lamb sacrificed for us. (See: Genesis 22:1–18; Leviticus 1:2–5; 1 Corinthians 5:7.)

Lambs were often sacrificed in Old Testament times—and Jesus, the best sacrifice of all, was called "the Lamb of God" (John 1:29).

The world's oldest person of modern times, Jeanne Calment of France, celebrates her 117th birthday. She was 122 when she died in 1997.

Eight Oldest People in the Bible:

1. Methuselah (969 years)
2. Jared (962 years)
3. Noah (950 years)
4. Adam (930 years)
5. Seth (912 years)
6. Kenan (910 years)
7. Enosh (905 years)
8. Mahalalel (895 years)

(See: Genesis 5:5, 8, 11, 14, 17, 20, 27; 9:29.)

I Love Lists!

Feature

ABRAHAM BATTLES FIVE INVADING KINGS

Abraham had such huge flocks and herds that he needed 318 servants to watch over them. Since Canaan was a wild land full of bandits and raiders, these shepherds were also trained fighters. Good thing they were! One day five foreign kings invaded eastern and southern Canaan and carried off loot and prisoners—including Abraham's nephew Lot. Abraham called his Amorite allies, and together they chased the kings, caught up with them, and scattered their armies in a stunning battle. They recovered Lot and the other prisoners, as well as all the goods and loot that those armies had taken. (See: Genesis 13:5–6; 14.)

FUN FACTS!
Conquering kings used to carry thrones around with them, and their officials lugged fancy seats along so they could sit in the gates of the cities that they conquered. (See: Jeremiah 1:15; 39:3.)

FUN FACTS!
Abraham and Isaac grazed their flocks in the Negev. Dangerous grazing! The Negev was "a land of. . . lions and lionesses, of adders and darting snakes" (Isaiah 30:6 NIV). (See also: Genesis 20:1; 24:62.)

Who's that?

ABIMELECH

Two kings of the Philistines were named Abimelech: One let Abraham and Sarah live in his city, Gerar, and the other let Isaac and Rebekah live there. Another Abimelech, an Israelite, was crowned king of Shechem. (See: Genesis 20; 26; Judges 9.)

FUN FACTS!
If you thought that Saul was the first Israelite to be king, you are mistaken. Abimelech was the first king in Israel. But all he ruled was the city of Shechem. (See: Judges 9:6.)

ABISHAG

The most beautiful woman in Israel. Abishag was brought to old King David to keep him warm in bed. Later, Prince Adonijah was killed for asking to marry her. (See: 1 Kings 1:1–4; 2:13–25.)

ABISHAI

King David's nephew and Joab's brother. Abishai was very loyal to David but cruel to his enemies. Abishai's solution was usually to kill people. (See: 1 Samuel 26:5–9; 2 Samuel 16:5–12; 1 Chronicles 2:16.)

Like Abishag, Shunit Faragi is the most beautiful Israeli woman of her time. She represented her country in the 2008 Miss Universe contest.

ANGELS

Angels are beings with supernatural powers who serve God and man. They bear His messages to mankind and protect believers. Angels were never human and people don't become angels when they die, but angels often look like humans when they appear. (See: Judges 13:3–6; Psalm 34:7; Luke 1:18–19; Hebrews 1:7, 14.)

And that Definition Means...

STRANGE BUT TRUE!
The astonishing thing about angels is that, although they're far mightier and more amazing than people, they're here to *serve* us! (See: Hebrews 1:7, 14; 2:6–7.)

The old Philistine city of Gaza is still around and often in the news. Smoke rises above buildings in this 2009 photo following an Israeli/Palestinian battle.

Places & People

Feature

PHILISTIA (PHILISTINES)

The Philistines ruled five cities—Gath, Gaza, Ekron, Ashdod, and Ashkelon—on the coast west of Israel. They were enemies of the Israelites for most of their history. (See: Joshua 13:3; Judges 13:1; 1 Samuel 31:1.)

CITIES BURIED BY BURNING SULFUR

The citizens of Sodom and Gomorrah were wealthy and were so oppressive that the poor cried out to heaven against them. On top of that, they had very dirty minds. When God sent two angels to Sodom, the people there tried to hurt them. That was it! At dawn the next day the angels dragged Lot and his family out of the city; then there was an ear-splitting roar and God rained scorching sulfur down on Sodom and the neighboring sinful cities. Thick black smoke rolled into the sky, and those wicked cities were gone. (See: Genesis 18:20–21; 19:1–29; Ezekiel 16:49–50.)

THE NAME GAME!

Shinab was the king of Admah, one of the cities destroyed along with Sodom and Gomorrah. This king had an odd name: *Shinab* means "father's tooth." (See: Genesis 14:2; Deuteronomy 29:23.)

Ten Times That People Lived in Caves

1. Lot and his daughters lived in a cave after the city of Sodom was destroyed.
2. The five Amorite kings who fled the Israelite army hid in the cave at Makkedah.
3. Israelites hid from the Midianites.
4. Samson stayed in a cave in the rock of Etam.
5. Israelite soldiers hid from the Philistines.
6. David and 400 men lived in the cave of Adullum.
7. David and his men hid in a cave at En Gedi.
8. Obadiah hid 100 prophets of God in two caves.
9. Elijah spent the night in a cave on Mount Sinai.
10. The poor in Job's day fled to caves.

(See: Genesis 19:24, 30; Joshua 10:16; Judges 6:2; 15:8; 1 Samuel 13:6; 22:1–2; 24:1–3; 1 Kings 18:4; 19:8–9; Job 30:3–6.)

I Love Lists!

Who's ?? that?

ABNER

The commander of King Saul's army. After Saul's death, Abner was about to unite the Israelites under David when Joab, David's nephew, killed him. (See: 2 Samuel 2–3.)

ABRAHAM

Father of the nation of Israel and spiritual father of those who believe in God. Abraham was 100 years old when his son Isaac was born. (See: Genesis 17:1–8; 21:5; Romans 4:1–16.)

FUN FACTS!
Once a ram was grazing on top of Mount Moriah when its curly horns were caught in a thicket. Abraham saw the ram, grabbed it, and sacrificed it to God. (See: Genesis 22:13.)

ABSALOM

A son of King David. He wanted to be king, so he gathered an army and fought his father—and died. Absalom was famous for his good looks and long hair. (See: 2 Samuel 14:25–26; 15–18.)

FUN FACTS!
When Prince Absalom wanted to be popular with the Israelites, he wouldn't let them bow down to him. Instead, he grabbed them and kissed them. (See: 2 Samuel 15:5–6.)

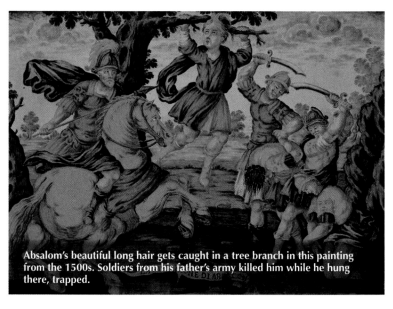

Absalom's beautiful long hair gets caught in a tree branch in this painting from the 1500s. Soldiers from his father's army killed him while he hung there, trapped.

And that Definition Means...

ALTAR OF BURNT OFFERING

A small platform that animals were sacrificed and burned on. Abraham, Elijah, and others built altars by piling rough stones together. God told the Israelites to build an altar of wood and cover it with bronze. When the temple was built in Jerusalem, the altar of burnt offering stood outside the temple's front doors. (See: Exodus 27:1–2; 1 Kings 18:30–32.)

Jesus talks with a woman from Samaria—a very unusual thing for a Jewish teacher to do. But He wants her to know the way to salvation.

Eight Famous Encounters at Wells and Pools

1. Abraham's servant, Eliezer, met Rebekah at the town well.
2. Philistine herdsmen drove Isaac away from two wells.
3. Jacob met his future wife, Rachel, at a well.
4. Moses drove nasty shepherds from a well in Midian.
5. Generals of two armies, Joab and Abner, met at the pool of Gibeon.
6. A woman once hid two of David's spies down in her well.
7. Jesus spoke with the Samaritan woman at Jacob's well.
8. Jesus healed a lame man at the Pool of Bethesda.

(See: Genesis 24:10–18; 26:19–22; 29:1–12; Exodus 2:15–21; 2 Samuel 2:12–16; 17:17–19; John 4:4–10; 5:1–8.)

Places & People

HEBREWS

Descendants of a man named Eber. Abraham was called a Hebrew, and so were his descendants. When the Hebrews lived in Egypt, they began to be called the children of Israel. (See: Genesis 11:16, 26; 14:13; Exodus 1:9.)

Seven Powerful Promises That God Made to Abraham

1. Abraham would be a blessing to everyone on earth.
2. God would give him the entire land of Canaan.
3. Abraham's offspring would be as numerous as the dust and the stars.
4. Abraham's descendants would be slaves 400 years, then be set free with great riches.
5. Abraham would live a long, peaceful life.
6. God would bless Ishmael and greatly increase his descendants—the Arabs.
7. His aged wife Sarah would miraculously have a son.

(Genesis 12:3; 13:14–17; 15:5, 13–15; 18–21; 17:20; 18:9–10,14.)

STRANGE BUT TRUE!
Anyone looking into Abner's tomb would've seen one skeleton but two skulls. Why's that? When Ish-bosheth (son of Saul) was beheaded, King David put his head in Abner's tomb. (See: 2 Samuel 4:12.)

ACHAN

Everything in the city of Jericho had been dedicated to God, but Achan took some treasure and clothes for himself, and this caused Israel to be defeated in Ai. Achan was killed for his sin. (See: Joshua 7.)

ADAM

The very first man. Adam was created by God, and he and Eve were the ancestors of all human beings. They lived in the Garden of Eden until they sinned. (See: Genesis 2–3.)

STRANGE BUT TRUE!

Energy-beam swords are not just science fiction! When the Garden of Eden was still on earth, God had a cherubim with a flaming sword guarding it. (See: Genesis 3:24.)

Adam and Eve cry after God kicks them out of the Garden of Eden in this painting from the 1400s.

ADONIJAH

When David was dying, Prince Adonijah declared himself king. Solomon became king instead, however. Adonijah was later killed for asking to have Abishag as his wife. (See: 1 Kings 1; 2:13–25.)

STRANGE BUT TRUE!

King Arthur wasn't the first king to have a round table. Two thousand years earlier, King Solomon had a *mesab*, which means "a circular, round table." (See: Song of Solomon 1:12.)

CURSE, THE

In the beginning, when God first created the earth and everything in it, "it was very good" (Genesis 1:31 KJV). After Adam and Eve sinned, however, God punished them. Not only did they begin to grow old and die, but God said, "Cursed is the ground because of you" (Genesis 3:17 RSV). That's when things like thorns and thistles and mosquitoes became problems. (See also: Genesis 2:17.)

FALL, THE

When God created Adam and Eve and placed them in the Garden of Eden, they were perfect and without sin, without death or sickness or anything evil. When they disobeyed God, however, they fell from that wonderful state and began to suffer from sin, death, and sickness. This is called the Fall. (See Curse, above.) Jesus will one day restore man's perfect state. (See also: Genesis 3:11–19; Revelation 21:4.)

Places & People

EDEN

No one knows exactly where the land of Eden was, though many people think it was in Iraq. God created a paradise there, the Garden of Eden, and Adam and Eve lived there. (See: Genesis 2:8–14.)

Feature

BAD BOYS BETRAY BRATTY BROTHER

Joseph was spoiled when he was young. He walked around in a fancy robe and drove his older brothers crazy by telling them that he dreamed they'd bow down to him one day. Just the same, Joseph didn't deserve what happened. One day, when they were far from home, Joseph's brothers decided to murder him. Fortunately, his oldest brother, Reuben, talked them out of it. Another brother, Judah, then had the "bright idea" of selling Joseph as a slave to a caravan headed down to Egypt—so they did. Then the brothers lied to their father Jacob that a wild animal had killed Joseph. (See: Genesis 37.)

FUN FACTS!
When Joseph first arrived in Egypt he was a slave. About 13 years later he was the master, and he made all the *Egyptians* slaves. (See: Genesis 37:36; 47:20–23.)

Five Thorn and Thorn-bush Names

Thorn bushes grew all over Israel. They were so common that parents named their kids after them:
1. *Soco* also means "thorny."
2. *Shamir* means "sharp point" or "thorn."
3. *Asnah* means "thorn bush."
4. *Hakkoz* means "thorn."
5. *Hassenaah* means "thorny."

I Love Lists!

(See: 1 Chronicles 4:18; 24:24; Ezra 2:50, 61; Nehemiah 3:3.)

Joseph, wearing only a cloth around his waist, is sold as a slave by his brothers. They hated Joseph for being their father's favorite.

Who's that?

AHAB

An idol-worshipping king of the northern kingdom, Israel. Ahab married Jezebel, the wicked princess of Sidon, and she pushed him into doing all kinds of evil things. (See: 1 Kings 16:29–33; 21.)

FUN FACTS!
Could you sit down and eat lunch if 450 false prophets had just been killed in front of you? King Ahab did. He must've had one tough stomach! (See: 1 Kings 18:19, 40–42.)

AHASUERUS

The Persian king who married Esther, a young Jewish woman. "Ahasuerus" (Esther 1:1 KJV) was very likely the Jews' name for the Persian king "Xerxes" (Esther 1:1 NIV). (See also: Esther 2:17.)

THE NAME GAME!
One of King Xerxes' servants had an unusual name—"Carcas" (Esther 1:10). That sounds a lot like *carcass*. And the odd thing is, his name means "vulture."

AHAZ

A king of Judah in the days of the Assyrian Empire. Ahaz paid the Assyrians gold to be on his side. Later, he made a copy of one of their pagan altars and worshipped on it. (See: 2 Kings 16.)

A Jewish boy dresses like King Ahasuerus for the holiday of Purim. Purim celebrates the Jews' escape from a plot to destroy them about 600 years before Jesus.

IDOL, IDOLATRY

And that Definition Means...

An *idol* is an object that supposedly represents an invisible god or goddess. Idols were usually made out of wood, stone, or metal and in the shape of humans or animals. *Idolatry* is the worship of these pagan gods and their idols, and God forbade idolatry. God mocked idols, saying that they were totally useless. (See: Exodus 20:3–4; Isaiah 44:9–20.)

Feature

FROM PRISON HOUSE TO POWERHOUSE

First Joseph's brothers hated him so much that they sold him as a slave. Talk about rejection! Joseph was a faithful, hardworking slave in Potiphar's house in Egypt but then Potiphar's wife falsely accused him of trying to hurt her. Potiphar was furious and threw Joseph in jail. There Joseph helped a prisoner, Pharaoh's wine taster, by interpreting his dreams. . .but when the man got out he forgot all about Joseph. When Joseph was about as low as he could get, suddenly he was called to the royal court to interpret Pharaoh's dream. Next thing you know, Joseph was the second most powerful man in Egypt. (See: Genesis 37, 39–41.)

FUN FACTS!
Joseph was 17 when he was sold as a slave into Egypt and 30 when he finally got out of prison. He'd been a slave and prisoner for 13 years. (See: Genesis 37:2, 36; 41:39–40, 46.)

Six Pagan Temples Right inside the Land of Israel

1. The temple of Baal in Shechem
2. The temple of Ashtoreth in Beth Shan
3. The temple of Baal in Samaria
4. The temple of Baal in Jerusalem
5. The temple of Dagon in Beth Shan
6. The Samaritans built a temple on Mount Gerizim. They first dedicated it to God, then rededicated it to Jupiter to please the Greeks.

(See: Judges 9:3–4; 1 Samuel 31:10; 2 Kings 10:23, 27; 11:18; 1 Chronicles 10:10; John 4:19.)

Eight Dramatic and Unusual Dreams

1. God told King Abimelech that he was basically dead meat.
2. In a dream, God told Laban to keep his mouth shut.
3. Joseph dreamed about sheaves of grain bowing down.
4. Pharaoh's wine taster and his baker had very odd dreams.
5. Pharaoh dreamed about cannibal cows.
6. A soldier dreamed about a giant barley cake smashing a tent.
7. Nebuchadnezzar dreamed about a tall, multi-metal statue.
8. An angel warned Joseph to escape with his family to Egypt.

(See: Genesis 20:3–7; 31:24; 37:5–7; 40:8–19; 41:17–21; Judges 7:13–15; Daniel 2:1, 31–35; Matthew 2:13.)

Many people around the world created idols. These wooden "tiki" carvings are from Hawaii.

Who's that?

AHAZIAH

A king of Judah. He was a son of wicked Queen Athaliah and worshipped Baal. Ahaziah was killed by Jehu while visiting his cousin, King Joram of Israel. (See: 2 Kings 8:25–29; 9:14–29.)

AMAZIAH

A king of Judah who worshipped God until he defeated the Edomites. Then he worshipped the Edomites' gods. He became proud and was defeated by King Jehoash of Israel. (See: 2 Chronicles 25.)

AMOS

A prophet of God in the days when Israel was prosperous. Amos preached against the selfish rich, warning them that God would judge them. (See: Amos 1:1; 6:1–7; 7:10–17.)

STRANGE BUT TRUE!
Another wicked man named Ahaziah, a king of Israel, was in the upper room of his palace where he fell through the wooden lattice and hit the ground, fatally injuring himself. (See: 2 Kings 1:2.)

And that Definition Means...

PROPHET, PROPHECY

A *prophet* was a man who gave a message from God. A female prophet was called a *prophetess*. Sometimes their prophecies simply warned that God would punish people if they didn't obey. Other times, prophets talked about things that would happen in the future. For example, Isaiah prophesied about Jesus' death and burial hundreds of years before Jesus was born. (See: Isaiah 53; Jeremiah 35:17.)

A chariot race is among the highlights of the 1959 movie *Ben-Hur*. Actor Charlton Heston (racing the white team) plays an angry man who meets Jesus and learns about forgiveness.

Five Deadly Chariot Rides

1. The Egyptian chariot army was drowned in the Red Sea.
2. Jabin's chariot army was wiped out in the River Kishon.
3. King Ahab was mortally wounded in a chariot.
4. Jehu killed King Joram with an arrow in his chariot.
5. King Ahaziah was mortally wounded in his chariot.

(See: Exodus 14:1–28; Judges 4:1–2, 14–15; 5:21; 1 Kings 22:34–35; 2 Kings 9:21–24, 27–28.)

Eight Queens— the Magnificent and the Misguided

1. Bathsheba, who sinned with King David, was the mother of King Solomon.
2. Zeruah, widow of a common man, was the mother of King Jeroboam.
3. Naamah, a foreigner from Ammon, was Solomon's queen and the mother of King Rehoboam.
4. Maacah, a goddess-worshipper, was Rehoboam's queen and the mother of King Abijah.
5. Azubah, a good Jerusalem girl, was Asa's queen and the mother of King Jehoshaphat.
6. Athaliah, one of history's nastiest women, was Jehoram's queen and the mother of King Ahaziah.
7. Zibiah, Ahaziah's queen, was the mother of godly King Joash.
8. Zebidah, good King Josiah's queen, was the mother of King Jehoiakim.

(See: 1 Kings 1:28–30; 11:26; 12:20; 14:21; 15:1–2, 13; 22:41–42; 2 Kings 8:25–26; 12:1; 23:36.)

Places & People

EDOM (EDOMITES)

Esau (Edom) was a son of Isaac. He conquered the land southeast of the Dead Sea and called it Edom. The Edomites often fought wars with Israel. (See: Genesis 25:30; Numbers 20:14–21.)

THE NAME GAME!

Talk about names with beautiful meanings! A man named *Me-Zahab* ("waters of gold") had a granddaughter named *Mehetabel* ("God is doing good"), the queen of Edom. (See: Genesis 36:39.)

FUN FACTS!

Queen Athaliah was the only woman to rule Judah, but she was so evil and outrageously wicked that it's fortunate she only reigned six years. (See: 2 Kings 11:1–3.)

Who's that?

ANDREW
One of the 12 apostles of Jesus. Andrew was Simon Peter's brother and, like Peter, used to be a fisherman and a disciple of John the Baptist. (See: Matthew 4:18–20; John 1:35–42.)

APOLLOS
Apollos was a highly educated Jew from Egypt. He was taught by Priscilla and Aquila in Ephesus, then became a leader in the church at Corinth. (See: Acts 18:24–28; 1 Corinthians 3:5–6.)

ARISTARCHUS
A little-known but faithful friend of the apostle Paul. Aristarchus was caught in a riot in Ephesus, then traveled with Paul to Greece, Jerusalem, and Rome. (See: Acts 19:1, 29; 20:1–4; 27:1–2.)

FUN FACTS!
Once some sailors tried to escape a doomed ship in a lifeboat, but the apostle Paul stopped them. Good thing! Otherwise all the passengers would've drowned. (See: Acts 27:30–32.)

And that Definition Means...

APOSTLE
Apostle means "messenger" or "ambassador." Jesus had about 120 disciples or followers, and from them He chose 12 to be His apostles. Jesus sent His apostles out to preach the gospel, perform miracles, and cast out demons. Later, other men such as Paul were called apostles, too. (See: Matthew 10:1–8; Luke 6:12–16; Acts 1:15; Ephesians 1:1.)

Lifeboats hang over the side of a ship, in case of trouble.

OBEDIENCE
The Bible talks a great deal about the importance of keeping (obeying) God's commands. The Jews were told that they would be blessed if they obeyed the Law of Moses and cursed if they disobeyed it. Jesus said, "If you love me, you will obey what I command" (John 14:15 NIV). (See also: Deuteronomy 28.)

STRANGE BUT TRUE!
God once told an army to dig ditches in the desert. It sounded strange—*very* strange—but they obeyed Him and won a huge battle as a result. (See: 2 Kings 3:15–24.)

Feature

DELIVERER JUMPS THE GUN

When Moses was a baby, he was adopted by Pharaoh's daughter. He was educated in all the wisdom of the Egyptians and became a powerful prince. When he learned that he was actually a son of Hebrew slaves, he went out to see how his people were doing. They were expecting a deliverer to come along about this time and set them free, so Moses figured (correctly) that he must be it. But in his haste he killed an Egyptian slave driver, and when Pharaoh found out, he tried to execute Moses. Moses had to flee into the desert and wait 40 years to be the deliverer—and *this* time he did things God's way. (See: Exodus 2; Acts 7:20–36.)

STRANGE BUT TRUE!

The archangel Michael once got in an argument with the devil. Guess what they were arguing about? The body of Moses! (See: Jude 1:9.)

Places & People

EPHESUS (EPHESIANS)

In Paul's day, Ephesus was a large city on the west coast of what is now Turkey. Paul preached the gospel there and a riot broke out. Paul later wrote a letter to the Ephesians. (See: Acts 19; Ephesians 1:1.)

Most Christians worship in church buildings today. But in the time of the apostle Paul, believers worshipped in each others' homes.

Four People Who Had Churches in Their Homes

1. Priscilla and Aquila in Rome
2. Priscilla and Aquila in Ephesus, Asia
3. Nympha in Colosse
4. Philemon in Colosse

(See: Romans 16:3–5; 1 Corinthians 16:19; Colossians 4:15; Philemon 2

I love Lists!

Who's that?

ASA

A king of Judah in the early days of the southern kingdom. Asa was a good king who got rid of idol-worship. He was constantly fighting with King Baasha of Israel. (See: 1 Kings 15:9–24.)

ASAPH

A Levite in the days of David and Solomon, he sang before the Ark of God and led praise services in the temple. He wrote 12 psalms. (See: 1 Chronicles 16:4–5; Psalms 50, 73–83.)

FUN FACTS!
King Solomon spent seven years building the temple of God. It took him 13 years—nearly *twice* as long!—to build his own magnificent palace. (See: 1 Kings 6:37–38; 7:1.)

ASHERAH

A disgusting goddess whom people believed was the wife of Baal. The Canaanites—and later the Israelites—worshipped her and set up "Asherah poles" (1 Kings 14:15 NIV). (See also: Judges 3:7.)

STRANGE BUT TRUE!
When Baal-worshippers *really* wanted their god to notice them and answer prayer, they slashed themselves with swords and spears till they were red with blood. (See: 1 Kings 18:26–28.)

And that Definition Means...

ARK OF THE COVENANT

Also called the Ark of God. The Ark was a gold-covered wooden chest with two golden cherubim on its lid. It was only three and a half feet long but it symbolized the presence of God. The Israelites stored special things inside the Ark, such as a jar of manna, Aaron's rod, and the stone tablets of the Ten Commandments. (See: Exodus 25:10–22; 1 Samuel 4:4, 11; Hebrews 9:3–5.)

STRANGE BUT TRUE!
Once a huge crowd of disrespectful men opened the lid of the Ark of the Covenant and looked inside—and God struck them dead, just like in the Indiana Jones movie! (See: 1 Samuel 6:19.)

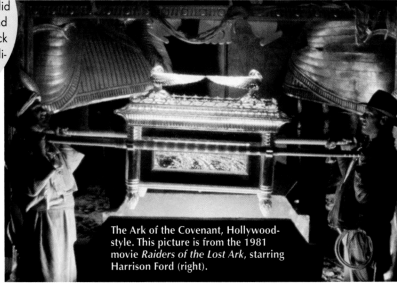

The Ark of the Covenant, Hollywood-style. This picture is from the 1981 movie *Raiders of the Lost Ark*, starring Harrison Ford (right).

Egyptians mummify the body of Joseph, as they had done with his father, Jacob, years before (Genesis 50:2).

Seven Asherah-Smashing, Baal-Bashing Heroes

1. Gideon tore down the Asherah pole and the altar of Baal.
2. The Israelites in Jephthah's day ditched their Baal and Asherah idols.
3. Elijah had the Israelites kill the prophets of Baal.
4. Jehu killed the prophets of Baal and demolished their temple.
5. In King Joash's day, the Israelites tore down the temple of Baal.
6. King Josiah burned Asherah poles and dumped the priests of Baal.
7. Asa destroyed idol altars, smashed sacred stones, and cut down Asherah poles.

(See: Judges 6:25–28; 10:6–7, 16; 1 Kings 18:19, 40; 2 Kings 10:23–27; 11:17–18; 23:4–6; 2 Chronicles 14:2–5.)

Feature

GREATER THAN THE MAGICIANS OF EGYPT

When Moses and Aaron appeared before Pharaoh, Aaron threw down Moses' staff, and it morphed into a snake. Pharaoh wasn't impressed. His court magicians did the same thing. Aaron struck the Nile, and all the water turned to blood. The magicians did the same. Aaron stretched his hand over the Nile, and swarms of frogs came out. The magicians summoned frogs, too. *Then* God caused gnats to fill the land. The magicians tried all their magic spells but couldn't do what God had done. They were also completely powerless to copy the next six plagues God sent on Egypt. (See: Exodus 7:8–12, 20–22; 8:5–7, 16–19.)

STRANGE BUT TRUE!

When Moses and the Israelites left Egypt, they were carrying a mummy with them—Joseph's embalmed body and bones. (See: Genesis 50:26; Exodus 13:19.)

23

Who's that?

ATHALIAH

The only ruling queen of Judah. When her son—King Ahaziah—died, evil, idolatrous Athaliah killed all of her grandsons (so she thought) so that she could become queen. (See: 2 Kings 11.)

FUN FACTS!
The Bible says about idols: "They have mouths, but they speak not, they have eyes, but they see not, they have ears, but they hear not" (Psalm 135:16–17 RSV). They're good for nothing!

BAAL

The chief pagan god of the Canaanites. Baal was supposedly the god of rain and crops and cattle. His followers had strange, sick ways of worshipping him. (See: 1 Kings 18:25–28.)

BAAL-ZEBUB

Baal-Zebub was originally a Philistine god. By Jesus' day, the Jews considered Beelzebub to be "the prince of demons" (Matthew 12:24 NIV), Satan himself. (See also: 2 Kings 1:2.)

FUN FACTS!
The Israelites worshipped an idol of a golden calf. Big mistake! But it was okay for them to make *statues* of 12 bulls because they didn't worship them. (See: Exodus 32; 1 Kings 7:25.)

This idol was made by Aztecs in South America more than 600 years ago.

And that Definition Means...

PASSOVER FEAST

In Egypt the angel of death "passed over" the houses of the Israelites who had put the blood of a lamb on their doorposts. God told the Israelites to celebrate the Passover Feast every year to remember what He had done for them. At this feast, the Jews ate lamb, unleavened (flat) bread, and bitter herbs. Jesus turned the Passover Feast into the Lord's Supper. (See: Exodus 12; Matthew 26:17–29.)

FUN FACTS!
When the Israelites left Egypt, hundreds of thousands of them carried containers of uncooked unleavened bread dough, wrapped in clothing, on their shoulders. (See: Exodus 12:33–34.)

FEAST OF UNLEAVENED BREAD

Leaven is an old word for *yeast*, which bakers mix into bread dough to make it rise. *Un*leavened bread is flat bread without yeast. The Feast of Unleavened Bread is a feast that lasted one week and followed immediately after Passover. In Jesus' day, the entire time was referred to as either Passover or the Feast of Unleavened Bread. Yeast symbolized evil and hypocrisy, and Paul wrote that Christians should be sincere and truthful. (See: Exodus 23:15; Matthew 26:17; 1 Corinthians 5:6–8.)

Feature

FOOLING AND FOILING PHARAOH

When Moses brought the Israelites out of Egypt, God led them south. . .then told them to head back north. It was a deliberate act to fool Pharaoh and make him think they were wandering around in confusion. Then God told the Israelites to camp by the Red Sea. He wanted it to look like they couldn't cross and were trapped. Pharaoh fell for it and sent his army after them. That night God opened up the Red Sea—a wall of water on the left hand and a wall on the right—and the Israelites safely crossed. When the Egyptians followed them into the seabed, however, the walls of water came crashing down and drowned them. (See: Exodus 13:17–14:31.)

AMMON (AMMONITES)

Ben-Ammi was a son of Lot, and his descendants, the Ammonites, lived in the land of Ammon east of the Jordan River. King David fought them. (See: Genesis 19:36–38; 2 Samuel 10:1–11:1; 12:26–31.)

Places & People

Six Pagan Gods the Israelites Foolishly Worshipped

1. Golden calves
2. Baal
3. Ashtoreth
4. Asherah
5. Molech, the god of the Ammonites
6. Chemosh, the god of Moab

I Love Lists!

(See: Exodus 32; Judges 2:11, 13; 3:7; 1 Kings 11:5, 7; 12:25–30.)

These carvings of the Egyptian pharaoh Rameses are more than 3,000 years old.

Who's that?

BALAAM

A prophet famous for owning a talking donkey. Balaam boasted that he saw visions from God, but he compromised with idol-worshippers for money. (See: Numbers 22; Jude 1:11.)

Balaam whips his donkey, unaware of the angel blocking the animal's path. God allowed the donkey to speak to Balaam, helping Balaam realize that he was in trouble with God.

FUN FACTS!
An Israelite named Caleb claimed his people could "swallow" their enemies. Balaam described the Israelites as a wild ox that "devour[s] hostile nations" (Numbers 24:8 NIV). (See also: Numbers 14:6–9.)

STRANGE BUT TRUE!
Some folks think that animals are more sensitive than people because Balaam's donkey saw an angel way before Balaam did. But then, Balaam's donkey could also *speak*! (See: Numbers 22:23–33.)

BALAK

The king of Moab in Moses' day. Balak was afraid of the Israelites camped on his border, so he offered Balaam great riches if he would come curse them. (See: Numbers 22:1–21; 24:10–11.)

BARABBAS

A notorious Jewish criminal. When Pilate said he'd release one prisoner at Passover, Jesus' religious enemies asked him to release Barabbas instead of Jesus. (See: Matthew 27:15–26; Mark 15:7.)

Actor Anthony Quinn plays Barabbas in a 1961 movie. In the story, Barabbas becomes a believer in Jesus—and is crucified during the Romans' persecution of Christians.

And that Definition Means...

LORD'S SUPPER

Jesus' final Passover meal with His disciples is called the Lord's Supper or the Last Supper. Jesus gave new meaning to this Passover meal when He told His disciples that drinking the wine was symbolic of drinking His blood (receiving salvation) and that eating the bread was symbolic of eating His body. We often call the Lord's Supper "communion." (See: Mark 14:12, 22–24.)

Feature

WAR AGAINST THE AMALEKITES

In Moses' day, fierce warlike nomads called Amalekites lived in the Sinai desert. When the Israelite slaves came out of Egypt with no fighting experience, the Amalekites attacked them. Moses stood on a nearby hill to watch the battle and held the staff of God over his head. As long as he held it up, the Israelites were winning. When he got tired and let it drop, the Amalekites started winning. Aaron and Hur realized what was happening, so they rolled a stone under Moses for him to sit on, then stood on either side of him, holding up his hands until sundown, and the Israelites won the battle. (See: Exodus 17:8–16.)

KADESH-BARNEA

Sometimes just called Kadesh, this oasis was in the desert south of Israel. It usually belonged to the Amalekites, but the Israelites lived there for many years. (See: Genesis 14:7; Numbers 20:1.)

Places & People

Nine Cases of Famous Folks Who Washed Their Faces, Hands, and Feet

1. The Lord and two angels washed their feet.
2. Eliezer and his men washed their feet.
3. Joseph's brothers washed their feet.
4. Joseph washed his face.
5. A Levite, his wife, and his servant washed their feet.
6. Bathsheba bathed in her enclosed courtyard.
7. Elisha used to help Elijah wash his hands.
8. Pilate washed his hands.
9. The Pharisees washed their hands often.

(See: Genesis 18:1–4, 16; 24:32; 43:24, 30–31; Judges 19:19–21; 2 Samuel 11:2; 2 Kings 3:11; Matthew 27:24; Mark 7:3–4.)

Four Times Animals Taught People a Thing or Two

1. Balaam's donkey rebuked him for his madness.
2. Job told his friends that the animals, the birds, and the fish could teach them.
3. The oxen knew their masters better than Israel knew God.
4. Birds knew better than God's people what they were supposed to do.

(See: Numbers 22:25–33; Job 12:7–8; Isaiah 1:3; Jeremiah 8:7.)

BARAK

When Jabin, a Canaanite king, conquered northern Israel, Deborah commanded Barak to fight Jabin, but Barak said he'd only go if she came with him—so she did. (See: Judges 4–5.)

BARNABAS

A leader in the early church. Barnabas was full of the Holy Spirit and very generous. He traveled around with the apostle Paul, preaching the gospel. (See: Acts 4:36–37; 11:19–25; 13.)

STRANGE BUT TRUE!
The main god of the Greeks was Zeus. Once, when Barnabas and Paul had healed a lame man in the city of Lystra, the people there thought that Barnabas was Zeus. (See: Acts 14:8–18.)

BARTIMAEUS

A blind man who begged by the roadside near Jericho. When Jesus passed by, Bartimaeus wouldn't stop calling out to Him, so Jesus healed him, giving him sight. (See: Mark 10:46–52.)

THE NAME GAME!
It's not kids' faults what their parents name them. One Christian in the New Testament was called *Nereus*. His folks had named him after a Greek sea god! (See: Romans 16:15.)

CONFESS

Confess means to speak out loud and tell others about something. The Bible says that we are to "confess. . . 'Jesus is Lord' " (Romans 10:9 NIV). This means to publicly speak about our faith in Jesus. We are also told: "confess your sins to each other" (James 5:16 NIV). That way, others can know to pray for us so that we can be healed.

ANAKIM AND OTHER GIANTS OF CANAAN

Goliath wasn't the only giant in the Bible. There were tons of other giants. In fact, there were *six entire nations* of giants. There were: **(1)** the Anakim of southern Canaan (Numbers 13:28, 33; Joshua 11:21); **(2)** the Rephaim of northern Canaan in the hill country of Ephraim (Joshua 17:15); **(3)** the Anakim of Gath and other cities on the coast (Joshua 11:22; 1 Samuel 17:4); **(4)** the Emim of Moab, east of the Dead Sea (Deuteronomy 2:9–11); **(5)** the Zamzummim of Ammon, east of the Jordan River (Deuteronomy 2:19–21); and **(6)** the Rephaim of Bashan, east of the Sea of Galilee (Genesis 14:5; Deuteronomy 3:4–5, 11).

Places & People

CANAAN (CANAANITES)

Noah cursed Canaan, a son of Ham. Canaan settled in the land of Canaan, which is now called Israel. His descendants, the Canaanites, were very wicked. (See: Genesis 9:20–25; Leviticus 18:24–25.)

FUN FACTS!

Once Israel did "more evil than the nations had done whom the LORD destroyed before the people of Israel" (2 Kings 21:9 RSV). God had kicked out the Canaanites. Now He kicked out the Israelites.

Four War Songs That Women Sang

1. Miriam led the women in a victory song over Pharaoh.
2. Deborah sang a song about defeating Jabin and Sisera.
3. Women sang about Saul and David defeating the Philistines.
4. Women sang sad songs about King Josiah's death following his defeat in battle.

(See: Exodus 15:20–21; Judges 5; 1 Samuel 18:6–7; 2 Chronicles 35:25.)

I Love Lists!

The Andrews sisters sang war songs to encourage Americans during World War II.

Who's that?

BARUCH

The son of a noble family and a close friend of the prophet Jeremiah. Baruch was Jeremiah's secretary and wrote down Jeremiah's prophecies. (See: Jeremiah 36:4; 45.)

BATHSHEBA

Bathsheba was married to one of David's warriors, Uriah the Hittite, but David had Uriah killed so that he could marry her. Bathsheba became the mother of Solomon. (See: 2 Samuel 11; 12:24.)

FUN FACTS!
The Bible says that Asahel, David's nephew, was "as fleet-footed as a wild gazelle" (2 Samuel 2:18 NIV). Not literally, of course. He was *fast*, but he couldn't run 50 miles an hour.

BELSHAZZAR

A descendant of Nebuchadnezzar, king of Babylon. King Belshazzar was feasting with a thousand nobles when a hand wrote a mysterious message on the palace wall. (See: Daniel 5.)

And that Definition Means...

SCRIBE

Originally, a *scribe* meant a professional letter-writer or secretary. Baruch was the prophet Jeremiah's scribe. Some scribes specialized in writing out copies of the Law of Moses, and they did it so much that they became really familiar with the Law. Eventually some scribes became teachers. Another name for *scribes* was "teachers of the law," and by Jesus' day, unfortunately, many of them were hypocrites (Matthew 23 NIV). (See also: Jeremiah 36:4.)

An elderly rabbi does the work of a scribe, fixing faded letters on a scroll of scripture.

THE BAD, MAD GRAB FOR LAND

When God told the Israelites to march into Canaan and take over the land, they decided to send spies in first. Fine. But when the spies came back with fearful stories, the people rebelled and decided *not* to march into Canaan. As punishment, they were told to wander in the desert 40 years until they all died. Then the Israelites decided that, well, they *would* invade after all. Moses said, "Do not go up, because the LORD is not with you" (Numbers 14:42 NIV), but they went anyway. They marched north, encountered the enemy, and. . .were completely defeated. (See: Numbers 13–14; Deuteronomy 1:19–35.)

FUN FACTS!
When the Israelites invaded Canaan, God told them to drive out all the Canaanites. They failed to do that, and years later the Canaanites ruled and mistreated them. (See: Judges 4:1–3.)

Places & People

BABYLON (BABYLONIANS)

Babylon was a gigantic city in what is now Iraq. It was the capitol of the Babylonian Empire. Its king, Nebuchadnezzar, conquered Judah and took the Jews to Babylon. (See: 2 Kings 25:1–11.)

FUN FACTS!
If you ever find a couple of cute little bear cubs and want to take them home, *forget* it! Don't even ask your mom. The mama bear will go absolutely wild. (See: 2 Samuel 17:8.)

FUN FACTS!
Talk about fast! Elijah once outran a horse-drawn chariot on a 20-mile run from Mount Carmel to the city of Jezreel—and it was pouring rain! (See: 1 Kings 18:44–46.)

Three Plagues Where Many People Died at Once

1. A small plague killed the 10 unbelieving spies.
2. A plague in the Israelite camp killed 14,700 people.
3. A plague killed 70,000 people throughout Israel.

(See: Numbers 14:37; 16:49; 1 Chronicles 21:14.)

Four Fearful, Snarling Bear Thoughts

Once, lots of Syrian brown bears lived in the forested hills of Israel and were a huge problem:
1. David killed a bear that was carrying off one of his sheep.
2. Two bears mauled a gang of 42 loud, mocking youths.
3. A mother bear robbed of her bear cubs will be furious.
4. God will tear apart the wicked like an angry she-bear.

(See: 1 Samuel 17:34–36; 2 Kings 2:23–24; Proverbs 17:12; Hosea 13:8.)

Who's that?

BENJAMIN

The youngest of Jacob's 12 sons. Rachel was the mother of Joseph and Benjamin and died giving birth to Benjamin. He was Joseph's favorite brother. (See: Genesis 35:16–18; 43:26–34.)

THE NAME GAME!
Joseph's brother Benjamin named two of his sons "Muppim" and "Huppim" (Genesis 46:21). That's *not* where the Muppets came from!

FUN FACTS!
When Joseph invited his 11 brothers to dinner, he gave his youngest brother, Benjamin, *five* times as much food as the others! Ben must've been stuffed! (See: Genesis 43:34.)

Kermit the Frog and Miss Piggy. . .no relation to the Bible's Muppim.

BEZALEL

A highly skilled craftsman in Moses' day. He worked in metals, wood, and stone and made the Ark of God and other items for the Tent of Meeting. (See: Exodus 31:1–11; 35:30–35.)

BOAZ

A rich farmer in Bethlehem and relative of Naomi. After Naomi's sons died, Boaz married Ruth, Naomi's daughter-in-law. Boaz was the great-grandfather of King David. (See: Ruth 2:1–12; 4:13–22.)

A modern craftsman, like the Bible's Bezalel, works on a piece of jewelry.

And that Definition Means...

TENT OF MEETING

Also called the *tabernacle* in the King James Bible. When the Israelites were wandering in the desert, they needed a place to keep the Ark of the Covenant and other holy objects. They also needed a place to worship God. God instructed Moses to build a large tent where He could meet with them. This tent had a large fence made of cloth around it. (See: Exodus 26; 29:42.)

Feature

GROUND AND FIRE GOBBLE UP GRUMBLERS

Once Korah, Dathan, and Abiram and 250 other Israelite leaders rose against Moses and Aaron. "Why have you set yourselves up as leaders?" they asked. "We're *all* holy!" Moses told everyone to appear before God the next day. When Korah and his followers showed up at the doorway of the Tent of Meeting, God warned all the Israelites to stand clear. As soon as everyone had moved a safe distance away, the ground opened up and swallowed Korah, Dathan, Abiram, and their households. Then fire scorched out from the Lord and burned up the 250 other rebels. After that it was *pretty clear* that God had chosen Moses and Aaron, not these other "holy" guys. (See: Numbers 16:1–35.)

FUN FACTS!
When millions of Israelites lived in cloth tents in the desert, you'd think fire was bound to break out in the tent camp sometime, right? Well, it did at least once. (See: Numbers 11:1–3.)

FUN FACTS!
When the Israelites lived 40 years in the desert, a pillar of cloud hovered over the Tent of Meeting. Each night it glowed like a pillar of fire. (See: Numbers 9:15–16.)

Five Times People Gave Clothing as Presents

1. Jacob gave his son Joseph a "coat of many colours" (Genesis 37:3 KJV).
2. Joseph gave his brother Benjamin five sets of clothes.
3. Samson gave his wedding guests 30 sets of clothing.
4. Naaman gave Gehazi, Elisha's servant, two sets of clothing.
5. A father gave his returning son the best robe he had.

(See: Genesis 45:22; Judges 14:19; 2 Kings 5:19–23; Luke 15:22.)

Three Famous Gatherings in the City Gates

Ancient cities were surrounded by walls, and elders often held important meetings in the busy gates:
1. Abraham talked to the Hittites in the gates of Hebron about buying a burial place.
2. Job often sat with the elders of Uz in the city gates, judging cases.
3. Boaz discussed buying Naomi's land and marrying Ruth in the gateway of Bethlehem.

(See: Genesis 23:1–11; Job 29:7–17; Ruth 4:1–11.)

Who's that?

CAESAR

Caesar was the last name of a leading Roman family and became a title of all Roman emperors. Caesar Augustus and Tiberius Caesar are mentioned in the New Testament. (See: Luke 2:1; 3:1.)

Tiberius Caesar

CAIAPHAS

Caiaphas was the high priest of Israel in Jesus' day. He was a selfish leader who sentenced Jesus to death to keep peace with the Romans. (See: John 11:47–50; Matthew 26:57–66.)

CAIN

The oldest son of Adam and Eve. Cain killed his brother Abel in a jealous rage, so God set a mark on Cain and made him a permanent wanderer. (See: Genesis 4:1–17.)

And that Definition Means...

HIGH PRIEST

The *high priest* was a man from the tribe of Levi who came before God to pray and to make sacrifices for the sins of his people. Moses' brother Aaron was the first high priest. When a high priest died, his son usually became high priest. Not all high priests were godly men; for example, Caiaphas condemned Jesus to death (See: Exodus 28:1; Numbers 20:25–28; Matthew 26:57–66).

The murderer Cain wanders the earth—his punishment from God—in this painting from 1880.

Feature

THE AMAZING BRONZE SERPENT

When the older, rebellious generation had all died, the young Israelites headed in to conquer Canaan. But as they were crossing the desert, they began complaining, "There is no water! And we detest this miserable food!" (Numbers 21:5 NIV). Then venomous snakes bit them and many Israelites died. When the people repented, God had Moses hammer a snake out of bronze and hold it up on a pole, and whoever looked at it was healed. Hundreds of years later, however, the Israelites began worshipping the bronze serpent as a god. Dumb mistake. King Hezekiah took a hammer and smashed it in pieces. (See: Numbers 21:4–9; 2 Kings 18:4.)

FUN FACTS!
When the Canaanites of Arad heard that the Israelites were passing by, they surprise-attacked them. Big mistake. The Israelites counter-attacked and wiped out their cities. (See: Numbers 21:1–3.)

The cottonmouth snake, found in the eastern United States, can kill with its venom.

Five Painful Snake Bites

1. Venomous snakes bit and killed Israelites in the wilderness.
2. "Whoever breaks through a wall may be bitten by a snake" (Ecclesiastes 10:8 NIV).
3. God threatened to send vipers to bite the evil Israelites.
4. Sometimes as men rested by a wall they were bitten by snakes .
5. Paul was bitten by a viper on Malta but suffered no ill effects.

(See: Numbers 21:4–9; Jeremiah 8:17; Amos 5:19; Acts 28:1-6)

STRANGE BUT TRUE!
The only people in the Bible who held conversations with animals were Eve, who chatted with a serpent; and Balaam, who argued with his donkey. (See: Genesis 3:1–5; Numbers 22:21–30.)

Places & People

CAESAREA
King Herod built a city with a good harbor on the northern coast of Israel. He named it after the emperor, Caesar, and the Romans made it the provincial capitol. Cornelius lived there. (See: Acts 10:1–2.)

AWESOME FEAT!
King Hezekiah wanted a secure water supply, so he had a tunnel cut through 1,700 feet of rock to bring water from a spring outside the city to a pool inside Jerusalem. (See: 2 Chronicles 32:30.)

Who's that?

CALEB

One of the 12 spies sent into Canaan. Only Caleb and Joshua brought back a good report. Many years later, at age 85, Caleb conquered the city of Hebron. (See: Numbers 13; Joshua 14:6–14.)

CORNELIUS

A Roman centurion who received a vision from God. Cornelius then asked Peter to come to his house and preach the gospel. Cornelius, his family, and his friends all became Christians. (See: Acts 10.)

FUN FACTS!
Tanners cleaned animal skins and made them into leather. They had a stinky job and their homes smelled. The apostle Peter stayed several days in a tanner's house. (See: Acts 9:43.)

CYRUS

The ruler of the Persian Empire who allowed the Jews to leave Babylon and return to Judah. Isaiah had prophesied about Cyrus hundreds of years earlier. (See: Ezra 1:1–4; Isaiah 45:1.)

A man dresses up like a Roman soldier of the apostle Peter's day.

And that Definition Means...

SYNAGOGUE

A Jewish house of worship. When the Babylonians destroyed the temple of God and took the Jews to far-off lands, the Jews began to meet together on Sabbaths and to pray and read and teach the Law. Eventually they built special buildings to do these things in. In Jesus' day, there were synagogues all over Israel—all over the Roman Empire, in fact. (See: Diaspora—below; see also: Luke 4:16; Acts 15:21.)

DIASPORA

The Jews living scattered among the Gentile nations. After the Jews were taken to Babylon, some returned home to Judea. Many others continued living in foreign nations, from Egypt to Persia to Greece. In Paul's day, there were Jews living in every major city of the Roman Empire. (See: Esther 8:9–17; John 7:35; Acts 15:21; James 1:1.)

Feature

THE DUDE WHO WAS DUMBER THAN HIS DONKEY

Balaam could hear from God yet he was buddy-buddy with idol-worshippers. He took the spiritual gifts of God lightly. So when the king of Moab called Balaam to put a curse on the Israelites and Balaam went, God sent an angel to kill Balaam. His donkey saw the angel and ran off into a field. Then she scraped against a wall to run past. Finally, she just lay down in the road. Balaam began beating her, and suddenly his donkey began speaking. Instead of cluing in that something unusual was happening, Balaam began arguing with his donkey. That's when the angel appeared to Balaam and laid things out plain—*real* plain. (See: Numbers 22:1–35.)

STRANGE BUT TRUE!
Once, Abraham stood under a tree and watched God and two angels eating lunch. Seriously! They had milk, curds, beef, and bread for the main course. (See: Genesis 18:6–8.)

FUN FACTS!
God said that the land of Canaan was a good land, but that the Canaanites who lived there were so wicked that the land would vomit them out. (See: Leviticus 18:28.)

Four Dusty, Desert Donkey Details

Thousands of years ago, tons of wild asses (donkeys) roamed the deserts near Canaan. Here's what the Bible says about them:
1. Hungry donkeys bray (call out) in the desert.
2. A wild donkey's colt can't be born as a man.
3. Poor people scrounge for food in the desert like wild donkeys.
4. Wild donkeys laugh at tame donkeys that have to work.

I Love Lists!

(See: Job 6:5; 11:12; 24:5; 39:5–8.)

Places & People

ROME (ROMANS)

Rome was the capital city of the Roman Empire. Paul was taken to Rome as a prisoner and preached the gospel there. He also wrote a letter to the Romans. (See: Acts 28:16–20; Romans 1:1–7.)

The apostle Paul probably recognized the Temple of Saturn in Rome—it was built 500 years before his time, and parts of it are still standing.

Who's that?

DAGON

A Philistine god. Samson destroyed Dagon's temple in Gaza. When the Ark of God was placed in Dagon's temple in Ashdod, his idol fell down before it. (See: Judges 16:21–30; 1 Samuel 5:1–4.)

STRANGE BUT TRUE!
The Philistines captured the Ark of the Covenant and put it in the temple of Dagon. The idol of Dagon fell over and lay flat before the Ark. They set Dagon up again, but he fell down again. (See: 1 Samuel 5:1–4.)

Many believe the Philistine god Dagon was like a male mermaid—half man and half fish.

DAMARIS

A Greek woman from Athens. When Paul preached to philosophers at the Areopagus (Mars' Hill), several men, as well as Damaris, became Christians. (See: Acts 17:19, 34.)

AWESOME FEAT!
When Samson lost his strength, the Philistines gouged out his eyes. When his strength returned, Samson killed 3,000 Philistines "for [his] two eyes" (Judges 16:28 NKJV). (See also: Judges 16:21–30.)

DANIEL

A Jewish youth taken as a prisoner to Babylon. After telling King Nebuchadnezzar his dream and interpreting it, Daniel became the king's chief adviser and the ruler over Babylon. (See: Daniel 1:1–6; 2.)

And that Definition Means...

CHRISTIAN

Those who believe in and follow Jesus Christ. In the book of Acts, *Christians* are usually referred to as "the believers" or "the disciples"—and "the disciples were called Christians first in Antioch" (Acts 11:26 KJV). To be a Christian begins with accepting Jesus as your Savior and Lord. Then you must obey and follow Jesus. (See: 1 John 2:6.)

FASTING

To go without food, or to avoid eating certain kinds of food. People fast to get their minds off of physical things and to focus on prayer to God. Daniel fasted for 21 days, eating "no delicacies" (Daniel 10:3 RSV). Jesus once fasted for 40 days. (See: Matthew 4:1–4.)

Feature

SPIES BENEATH THE PILES OF FLAX

One time, Joshua sent two spies into Jericho to check out the city's defenses, but they were spotted. The spies ducked into the house of a sinful woman named Rahab, but the king sent soldiers there to arrest them. Rahab had a linen-making business (linen threads come from the flax plant), and she had flax drying on the flat roof of her house. Quickly, Rahab took the men up onto her roof and covered them with heaps of flax. The soldiers searched but didn't find them, and thanks to Rahab's sending the soldiers another direction, the two spies then escaped and took their report back to Joshua. (See: Joshua 2.)

FUN FACTS!
Many Israelites lived east of the Jordan River, and when the men went off to war, they left their families behind—and didn't see them for five or six years! (See: Numbers 32:1–6, 16–18; Joshua 22:1–4.)

FUN FACTS!
A clan of Israelites living in the town of Beth Ashbea specialized in growing crops of flax and weaving their threads into linen clothes. (See: 1 Chronicles 4:21.)

Olives were an important crop for people of biblical times.

Seven Famous and Somewhat Fantastic Trees

1. The tree of life
2. The tree of the knowledge
3. The great tree of Moreh—also called the soothsayers' tree
4. The great oaks of Mamre
5. The olive tree that refused to be king
6. The cedar treetop transplanted by an eagle
7. The enormous tree in King Nebuchadnezzar's dream

(Genesis 2:9; 3:1–7, 22; 12:6; 13:18; 14:13; Judges 9:8–9, 37; Ezekiel 17:1–4; Daniel 4:10–12; Revelation 2:7; 22:2.)

I Love Lists!

Who's that?

DARIUS

King Darius the Mede was an ally of the Persians, and his army conquered the city of Babylon. Darius was tricked into throwing Daniel into the lions' den. (See: Daniel 5:30–31; 6.)

STRANGE BUT TRUE!
God sent an angel with the answer to Daniel's prayer, but a demon prince blocked him for 21 days. Finally the archangel Michael helped the angel break through. (See: Daniel 10:12–13.)

DAVID

David was a shepherd when he was a youth in Bethlehem. He later became King Saul's musician and bodyguard, then became the second king of Israel. (See: 1 Samuel 16; 2 Samuel 5:1–5.)

FUN FACTS!
The Israelites beat grain to break off the covering (chaff), then tossed the grain in the air to let the wind blow the chaff away. David prayed that his enemies would be like chaff. (See: Psalm 35:4–5.)

FUN FACTS!
In King Saul's day, there were no blacksmiths in Israel. Then, 400 years later, there were no blacksmiths in Israel again. They all went off to Babylon. (See: 1 Samuel 13:19; 2 Kings 24:14.)

David ruins his rule as Israel's king by stealing his neighbor's wife, Bathsheba. When he should have been out fighting a battle, he stayed home—and saw the beautiful woman bathing next door (see 2 Samuel 11).

DEBORAH

A prophetess and a judge of Israel. When Jabin, a Canaanite king, invaded Israel, Deborah commanded Barak to defeat Jabin. Afterward she wrote a famous battle song. (See: Judges 4–5.)

JUDGMENT

And that Definition Means...

A decision or ruling by judges and rulers. When he was king of Israel, "David executed judgment and justice" (2 Samuel 8:15 KJV). *Judgment* also means God's decision or ruling on a matter: "The judgments of the LORD are true and righteous" (Psalm 19:9 NKJV). *Judgment* also means a disaster God sent upon people to punish them, such as when God judged Sodom. (See: Genesis 19:24–25.)

GREAT WHITE THRONE OF JUDGMENT

The final Judgment at the end of the world when God will judge the unsaved. (Believers are judged earlier at the "judgment seat of Christ," see page 140.) (See also: Revelation 20:11–15)

Feature

THE DAY A FLOODING RIVER DRIED UP

The Jordan River is normally not wide or deep, but when the snow melts and rains fall in spring, it overflows its banks onto a flood plain nearly a mile wide. And *this* was the time God picked for the Israelites to cross. They had no way of knowing, but it seems that hours earlier a landslide had blocked the river 20 miles upstream at a town called Adam. Talk about miraculous timing! The instant God's priests walked into the water, the last of the water ran past and the river dried up! The dam held *just* long enough for all the Israelites to cross over, then the water broke out and the river flooded again. (See: Joshua 3–4.)

FUN FACTS!
When God dried up rivers and seas, two things happened: (1) the Israelites crossed on dry land, and (2) the stranded fish died and rotted. (See: Exodus 14:21–22; Joshua 3:15–17; Isaiah 50:2.)

Ten Prophetesses (Lady Prophets)

1. Miriam
2. Deborah
3. Huldah
4. Noadiah—she was a bad one!
5. Isaiah's wife
6. Anna
7–10. Philip's four daughters

(See: Exodus 15:20; Judges 4:4; 2 Kings 22:14; Nehemiah 6:14; Isaiah 8:3; Luke 2:36–38; Acts 21:9.)

I Love Lists!

Places & People

JORDAN RIVER

This river flows south from the Sea of Galilee into the Dead Sea, and formed the eastern border of Canaan. The Israelites crossed it during flood season, and John baptized people there. (See: Joshua 3:14–17; Matthew 3:4–6).

Judgment—in the form of legal decisions—is often shown as a woman holding a scale.

Who's that?

DELILAH

A Philistine woman whom Samson loved. The Philistine lords offered Delilah money to betray Samson, so she pestered him until he told her the secret of his strength. (See: Judges 16:4–21.)

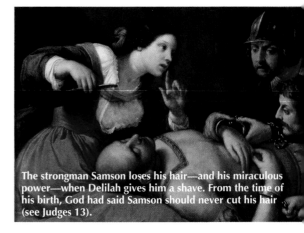

The strongman Samson loses his hair—and his miraculous power—when Delilah gives him a shave. From the time of his birth, God had said Samson should never cut his hair (see Judges 13).

STRANGE BUT TRUE!
Samson could kill a lion with his bare hands and rip off city gates without getting tired. But Delilah's constant nagging made him "tired to death" (Judges 16:16 NIV). (See also: Judges 14:5–6.)

DEMAS

When Paul was in prison, Demas was one of his closest helpers. Later on, however, Demas "loved this present world" (2 Timothy 4:10 NKJV) and deserted Paul. (See: Philemon 1:23–24.)

DEMETRIUS

A silversmith in Ephesus who made silver shrines of the goddess Artemis (Diana). Demetrius started a riot when Paul taught that manmade gods were not real. (See: Acts 19:23–41.)

And that Definition Means...

DAY OF ATONEMENT

One day a year, the high priest would go into the Holy of Holies with the blood of a goat to atone for the sins that the Israelites had committed in ignorance. This day was called Yom Kippur or the Feast of Atonement—even though they fasted on this day. (See: Atonement and Holy of Holies, both found on page 46.) God then covered the sins of the Israelites and forgave them. (See: Leviticus 16; Hebrews 9:7–8.)

SCAPEGOAT

On the Day of Atonement, the high priest took two goats: the first goat was sacrificed (killed). The high priest then symbolically placed the sins of the nation on the second goat. Then the scapegoat (*escape*-goat) was driven out into the wilderness. These days a scapegoat means anyone who is picked out and blamed for other people's mistakes. (See: Leviticus 16:1–22.)

STRANGE BUT TRUE!
People once believed in satyrs (half-goat, half-human beings), so when they read that the *sair* danced in ruined cities, they thought the Hebrew word *sair* meant *satyr* (Isaiah 13:21 KJV).

A camouflaged soldier waits in ambush.

Five Ambushes from Bushes and Buildings

1. The Israelites ambushed the Canaanite city of Ai.
2. The Israelites ambushed the Benjamites in Gibeon.
3. The king of Aram tried to ambush the king of Israel several times.
4. King Jeroboam's armies ambushed King Abijah's army.
5. More than 40 men waited to ambush the apostle Paul.

(See: Joshua 8:12; Judges 20:28–29; 2 Kings 6:8–10; 2 Chronicles 13:13–15; Acts 23:20–21.)

Feature

TINY CITY A HARD NUT TO CRACK

After God had helped them win a great victory at Jericho, the Israelites came to the city of Ai (*Ay*-eye). Since the city was so small, Joshua sent only 3,000 soldiers against it. To everyone's surprise, the men of Ai came rushing out, killed 36 Israelites, and drove the rest of Israel's army off. Joshua was stunned. Why hadn't God helped them win such an easy battle? Then he found out why. All the treasures of Jericho were supposed to have been given to God, but an Israelite named Achan had kept some for himself. He had stolen from God! When the Israelites dealt with *that* sin, then God helped them defeat Ai. (See: Joshua 7:1–8:29.)

AWESOME FEAT!
Ox goads were long poles with a metal point for poking lazy oxen. A superhero named Shamgar once killed 600 Philistines with an ox goad. (See: Judges 3:31.)

Who's that?

DINAH

A daughter of Jacob and Leah. The Canaanite prince of Shechem hurt her, then spoke kindly to her and wanted to marry her. Dinah's brothers killed all the men in Shechem in revenge. (See: Genesis 34.)

FUN FACTS!
There are 66 names in a list of Jacob's descendants. The only females included in this all-boy list are his two granddaughters, Dinah (Genesis 46:15) and Serah (Genesis 46:17). (See also: Genesis 46:8–26.)

EBED-MELECH

An Ethiopian (Cushite) official in King Zedekiah's court. When he learned that Jeremiah had been cast into a mud-filled pit, he got permission to rescue him. (See: Jeremiah 38:1–13.)

ELEAZAR

The third son of Aaron. Eleazar became chief priest after Aaron's death. He helped Joshua divide the land of Canaan among the tribes of Israel. (See: Exodus 6:23; Numbers 20:28; 34:17.)

And that Definition Means...

AVENGE, AVENGER

In ancient times when someone killed a person, a man in the dead person's family would kill the murderer to get even. He was the avenger. God says that He will avenge us when people hurt or persecute us, so we are to love our enemies and not to take vengeance on them ourselves. (See: Numbers 35:14–25; Romans 12:19–21.)

Feature

WACKY, WEIRD WEATHER AT WAR

Once five Amorite kings attacked Israel's allies, the Gibeonites, so Joshua marched his army to Gibeon by night and surprised the Amorites early the next morning. The Amorites were so panicked that they took off running down the road. The Israelites chased them and began cutting them down. Then weird, wild, weather broke loose. The sky grew dark with storm clouds, and God began hurling down huge, baseball-sized hailstones on the terrified Amorites. More Amorites died from being hit by hailstones than were killed by the swords of the Israelites. (See: Joshua 10:1–11.)

FUN FACTS!
When the King James Bible asks, "Hast thou entered into the treasures of the snow?" it's *not* asking, "Have you been to Santa Claus's toy factory at the North Pole?" (See: Job 38:22.)

God bombed Amorite soldiers with hailstones like these during a battle against Joshua.

Millstones are grooved to help grind grain into flour.

Eight Weird War Weapons

1. The Red Sea parted, then washed back, drowning the Egyptians.
2. Giant hailstones wiped out the Amorite armies.
3. Swarms of angry hornets drove the Canaanites out of Canaan.
4. A woman dropped a millstone on King Abimelech's head.
5. Samson used the jaw bone of a donkey as a weapon.
6. God caused loud thunder to panic the Philistines.
7. Forest trees killed King David's enemies.
8. God caused the loud, fake noise of an army attacking, which sent the Arameans fleeing.

(See: Exodus 14:21–28; Joshua 10:11; 24:12; Judges 9:52–53; 15:14–16; 1 Samuel 7:10; 2 Samuel 18:6–8; 2 Kings 7:5–7.)

I love Lists!

Places & People

CUSH (CUSHITES)

Cush was a kingdom south of Egypt, in the land that is today called Sudan. Candace was queen of Cush (sometimes mistakenly called Ethiopia) in New Testament times. (See: Acts 8:26–27.)

FUN FACTS!
The kings and armies of Judah had a secret escape route out of Jerusalem. In King Zedekiah's day, it was a secret gate in the palace garden, between the two city walls. (See: 2 Kings 25:2–4.)

FUN FACTS!
Jacob's body was brought from Egypt and buried in Mamre. His son Joseph's bones were brought from Egypt and buried in Shechem, a different city. (See: Genesis 50:13–14; Joshua 24:32.)

Who's that?

ELI

A later descendant of Aaron and a high priest. Eli's sons were wicked, and he didn't control them, so God took away his family's right to be high priests. (See: 1 Samuel 2:11–36.)

ELIEZER

Abraham's steward (overseer of his belongings). Eliezer was most likely the servant who went to Haran to find a wife for Abraham's son Isaac. (See: Genesis 15:2; 24:1–67.)

ELIJAH

A prophet of Israel (the northern kingdom) in the days of King Ahab. Elijah called for a drought on the land and called fire down from heaven. (See: 1 Kings 17:1; 18:36–38; 2 Kings 1:7–12.)

STRANGE BUT TRUE!
The prophet Elijah apparently started the trend of dressing in animal-hair robes. Hundreds of years later, prophets still dressed that way. (See: 2 Kings 1:7–8; Mark 1:6.)

Elijah (center) watches fire from heaven burn up the sacrifice he put on the altar to God. Meanwhile, priests of the false god Baal dance around their altar, trying to get a similar response.

HOLY OF HOLIES

And that Definition Means...

Also called the Most Holy Place. It was a small room in the heart of the temple where the Ark of the Covenant was kept, and where God's presence was. A thick curtain kept the people out. Once a year on the Day of Atonement, the high priest entered this room to pray for God to forgive the sins that the people had done in ignorance. (See: Exodus 26:31–35; Leviticus 16; Hebrews 9:1–8.)

ATONE, ATONEMENT

A Bible translator invented the word *atone* (at-one) to show how Jesus makes peace between us and God. Sin separates us from God, but when Jesus died on the cross, He *atoned* for our sins. He made us "at one" with God. *Kaphar*, which is the Hebrew word for *atone*, means "to cover." Jesus' blood covers our sins. (See: Exodus 30:10; 32:30; Romans 3:23; 6:23.)

Feature

SURPRISE ATTACK ON HAZOR

After God helped the Israelites defeat the Amorite kings down south, the Canaanites of the north became alarmed. Normally, all their little cities and kingdoms fought among themselves, but now Jabin, king of Hazor, sent out word to all the kings of the north, and they gathered to fight Israel. Joshua didn't wait for this monster army to march south. He quickly marched his army north, caught the Canaanites before they were ready, and obliterated their armies—all in one blow! Then with the soldiers of Hazor and the other cities gone, Joshua was able to easily capture their unguarded cities. (See: Joshua 11:1–15.)

Places & People

AMORITES

Thousands of years ago, desert tribes called Amorites settled in Canaan. Abraham was friends with them. Later the Amorites became wicked and Joshua battled them. (See: Genesis 14:13; Joshua 10:5–10.)

FUN FACTS!

When the false god Baal didn't answer his prophet's prayers, Elijah mocked them saying, "Shout louder! . . . Maybe he is sleeping and must be awakened" (1 Kings 18:27 NIV).

THE NAME GAME!

When God told Abraham that his 90-year-old wife Sarah would have a baby, Abraham fell to the ground laughing—so God told him to name his son *Isaac*, meaning "he laughs." (See: Genesis 17:15–19.)

Three Fattest Men in the Bible

1. Eglon king of Moab was a "very fat man" (Judges 3:17 NKJV). (See also: Judges 3:21–22.)
2. Eli was so "heavy" (1 Samuel 4:18 RSV) that he died when he fell off his chair.
3. Regarding rich men, Psalm 73:7 (KJV) says, "Their eyes stand out with fatness."

I love Lists!

Six Times Fierce, Miraculous Fire Fell

1. Fire came out from the Lord and killed 250 rebellious men.
2. The fire of the Lord fell on Elijah's sacrifice on Mount Carmel.
3–4. Elijah called down fire *two times* to kill 100 men.
5. God sent down fire from heaven on David's sacrifices.
6. God sent down fire when Solomon dedicated the temple.

(See: Numbers 16:35; 1 Kings 18:38; 2 Kings 1:9–12; 1 Chronicles 21:26; 2 Chronicles 7:1.)

Who's that?

ELISHA

A prophet who worked closely with Elijah and inherited his cloak when he was caught up into heaven. Elisha did even more miracles than Elijah. (See: 1 Kings 19:19–21; 2 Kings 2:1–22.)

FUN FACTS!
Ever had someone stare at you so long that you wondered what you did wrong? The prophet Elisha stared at Hazael so long that Hazael was ashamed. (See: 2 Kings 8:10–11.)

STRANGE BUT TRUE!
The only time the Bible talks about anybody sneezing is when it mentions that a young boy sneezed seven times in a row—after Elisha brought him back to life! (See: 2 Kings 4:35.)

ENOCH

A godly man who lived before the Flood. Enoch "walked with God" (Genesis 5:22 KJV), and when he was 365 years old, God took him to heaven—alive! Enoch didn't even die. (See: Genesis 5:18–24.)

EPAPHRAS

The apostle Paul's "dear fellow servant" (Colossians 1:7 NIV) and the minister of the church at Colosse. He was always praying for God to help his fellow Christians. (See: Colossians 4:12–13.)

THE NAME GAME!
Epaphras was the faithful Christian minister of the church of Colosse. But what a name for people to call you all day long! *Epaphras* means "handsome" or "charming." (See: Colossians 1:7.)

And that Definition Means...

CHURCH

The Greek word for "church" is ekklēsia, which means the community of believers "called out" from the world to follow Jesus. When Paul preached the gospel in a new city, one of the first things he did was to organize fellowships of new believers—churches. The church is Christ's body here on earth, representing Him to the world. (See: Body of Christ, page 130; see also Acts 14:21–23.)

HEAVEN

A place of perfect peace, health, and joy that lasts forever. The saved will live in heaven in the presence of God, Jesus, and the holy angels. Right now, heaven is a spiritual place only, but one day God will come down to a new earth to dwell with people. Heaven will then be a supernatural spiritual/physical place on earth. (See: Revelation 7:15–17; 21:1–7, 12.)

King Solomon uses his wisdom to figure out which woman is the mother of a living child. Read the whole story in 1 Kings 3:16–28.

Two Arguments over Babies

There are two times in the Old Testament where two women each had a baby; one baby died and one baby was alive, and the women argued about the living baby.

1. In King Solomon's day
2. In the prophet Elisha's day

(See: 1 Kings 3:16–27; 2 Kings 6:26–30.)

I Love Lists!

Feature

ROOTING OUT THE FOREST GIANTS

In Joshua's day, the hills of Canaan were covered with thick forests. The Canaanites lived down in the fertile plains and had speedy chariot armies. Now, when the Israelites entered Canaan, members of the tribe of Manasseh complained that there were so *many* of them that they had no room to live. Okay then. Joshua gave them a choice: either fight the chariot armies in the plains or pick up their axes, go up into the hills, and clear some farmland. The people of Manasseh chose the forests. They had to fight the giants (Rephaim) living up in the hills, but it must've beat dodging iron chariots. (See: Joshua 17:14–18.)

REALLY GROSS!

These days, people wash their cars to make them look nice and shiny. In Israel, men washed their chariots when they were bloody from battle. (See: 1 Kings 22:37–38.)

Who's that?

EPAPHRODITUS

When Paul was in prison, the Christians of Philippi sent Epaphroditus with money to help him. While he was in Rome, Epaphroditus became so sick that he nearly died. (See: Philippians 2:25–29.)

ESAU

The son of Isaac, and Jacob's twin brother. Esau was the oldest brother but didn't really care for his birthright, so he sold it to Jacob for a bowl of stew and some bread. (See: Genesis 25:21–34.)

STRANGE BUT TRUE!
Esau was so incredibly hairy that to run your fingers along his arm was about the same as petting a goat. *Seriously!* (See: Genesis 27:11–16, 21–23.)

ESTHER

A beautiful Jewish woman living in the capital of Persia. When King Ahaseurus (Xerxes) needed a new queen, he picked Esther. She later saved her people from being killed. (See: Esther 2:17; 7–8.)

A young Jewish girl dresses as Queen Esther for a Purim celebration.

And that Definition Means...

BIRTHRIGHT

In Israel, the firstborn son received the birthright—the right to a double share of his father's property. The firstborn Esau traded his huge birthright to his younger brother, Jacob, for one bowl of stew. The Prodigal Son was not the oldest son, so he received a smaller inheritance—fortunately, since he wasted it! (See: Genesis 25:24–34; Deuteronomy 21:15–17; Luke 15:11–13.)

Feature

SEVENTY KINGS SCRAPPING FOR SCRAPS

When the Israelites came into Canaan, they had to deal with some very nasty characters. Take Adoni-Bezek, for example: He was the Canaanite king of Bezek, and he constantly made war against neighboring cities. Whenever he captured a king, he cut off his thumbs and big toes and kept him as a prisoner. Only dogs ate scraps that fell from the table, but to humiliate the conquered kings, Adoni-Bezek forced them to fight for food and scramble for scraps under his palace table. That was one *huge* mess of scraps! No wonder the Israelites cut off Adoni-Bezek's big toes and thumbs. (See: Matthew 15:27; Judges 1:1–8.)

FUN FACTS!
Two rulers Adoni-Zedek, a king of Jerusalem, and Adoni-Bezek, a king of Bezek fought the Israelites. Betcha can't say "Adoni-Zedek and Adoni-Bezek" real fast ten times. (See: Joshua 10:1–10; Judges 1:4–6.)

Places & People

PHILIPPI (PHILIPPIANS)

Philippi was one of the most important cities of Macedonia (northern Greece). Paul preached the gospel there and later wrote a letter to the Philippians. (See: Acts 16:11–12; Philippians 1:1.)

FUN FACTS!
The ancient Persians had a Pony Express. They had an excellent road system, and when they had urgent messages, they sent messengers on the swiftest horses. (See: Esther 8:10, 14.)

The first person martyred (killed for following Jesus) is Stephen, stoned by people who hated his preaching (Acts 6:8–7:60).

Four Mentions of Ridden Horses

1. The royal horses of Persian messengers
2. The warhorses of Uz
3. The mount of the apostle Paul
4. White horses of Jesus and the armies of heaven

(See: Esther 8:14; Job 39:19–25; Acts 23:23–24; Revelation 19:11–14.)

Five Very Tough Punishments

1. Burning—for a man who marries a woman and her mother
2. Stoning—for being a medium, for blasphemy, for gathering wood on the Sabbath, for idolatry
3. Throwing captured enemy soldiers off a cliff
4. Hanging—of Haman, who had built the gallows for Esther's cousin Mordecai
5. Sawing people in two

(See: Leviticus 20:14, 27; 24:16; Numbers 15:32–36; Deuteronomy 13:6–10; 2 Chronicles 25:12; Esther 7:9–10; Hebrews 11:37.)

Who's **?** that?

EVE

The first woman and the wife of Adam. Eve was created from one of Adam's ribs. Satan, as a serpent, convinced her to disobey God and eat the forbidden fruit. (See: Genesis 2:20–3:24.)

EZEKIEL

A prophet who lived in Babylon and had some of the most bizarre visions in the Bible. Ezekiel also did some very odd things in order to obey God. (See: Ezekiel 1:3–28; 4:1–17; 12:1–7; 37:1–14.)

STRANGE BUT TRUE!
Ezekiel once had a vision of a valley filled with dry bones. There was a tremendous rattling and clanking when the skeletons suddenly reassembled! (See: Ezekiel 37:1–10.)

FUN FACTS!
Ezekiel was some prophet! God told him to dig through the temple wall to get into the temple. Later, God told Ezekiel to dig through the wall of his house to get out. (See: Ezekiel 8:7–8; 12:5–7.)

EZRA

A wise scribe who traveled from Babylon to Judah to teach the Law of Moses to the Jewish people. Ezra spoke strongly against Jews marrying nonbelievers. (See: Ezra 7; 9–10.)

And that Definition Means...

ORIGINAL SIN

The original (very first) sin was when Adam and Eve disobeyed God and ate the fruit of the tree of the knowledge. This brought the curse and death into the world. Adam and Eve then had sinful natures, and all humans after them did as well. (See Curse, page 14, and Sinful Nature, page 132; see also: Genesis 3; 1 Corinthians 15:21–22.)

In one of the creepiest scenes in the Bible, the prophet Ezekiel watches a bunch of old skeletons come back to life.

Feature

OUTWITTING SISERA'S CHARIOT ARMY

When the Israelites took over Canaan, they didn't finish driving out the Canaanites. Big mistake. Several years later, the Canaanite king, Jabin, overran northern Israel. His general, Sisera, had 900 chariots and cruelly crushed the Israelites for 20 years. The Israelites had no chariots. What to do? God set a trap: He had the Israelites lure Sisera's army into the flat Kishon River valley. Sisera was delighted. This was an ideal chariot battlefield. But then a sudden rainstorm broke, the river overflowed its banks, and his chariots were useless in the mud. The Israelites wiped out the entire Canaanite army. (See: Judges 4:1–16; 5:4, 21.)

FUN FACTS!
God said that He could've helped Israel drive out the Canaanites in one year, but He didn't do it, or the land would have quickly filled up with wild animals. (See: Exodus 23:27–29.)

Places & People

JUDAH

After Solomon died, the nation of Israel split into two kingdoms—the northern tribes were called Israel, and the southern tribe, Judah, was called Judah. Many years later the Romans called the land *Judea*. (See: 1 Kings 12:16–20; Matthew 2:1.)

A Christian rock group, Stryper, was known as a "hair band." Can you guess why?

Six Men and Their Hair

1. Esau was completely covered with hair when he was born.
2. When Samson's hair was cut, he lost his strength.
3. Absalom had such long hair that it weighed five pounds.
4. Ezekiel cut off all his hair and burned some of it.
5. Nebuchadnezzar, a king of Babylon, had hair that was long, dirty, and matted together.
6. Ezra pulled some of his hair out in grief.

(See: Genesis 25:24-25; Judges 16:17–20; 2 Samuel 14:25–26; Ezekiel 5:1–4; Daniel 4:33; Ezra 9:3.)

I love Lists!

Who's ??? that?

FELIX

The Roman governor of Judea. When Paul's Jewish enemies accused Paul of crimes, Felix didn't hand Paul over to them—but he didn't set Paul free either. (See: Acts 24.)

This bronze coin is from the time of Felix.

FUN FACTS!
The Roman governor Felix was afraid of the gospel message, but often talked with Paul because he hoped that Paul would offer him a bribe. Paul didn't, by the way. (See: Acts 24:25–26.)

FESTUS

Festus replaced Felix as governor. When Paul insisted on being judged by Caesar, Festus held a court hearing first to find out from Paul exactly what had happened (Acts 24:27; 25–26).

GABRIEL

A high-ranking angel who often took messages to Israel. He made announcements to Daniel, to Zechariah, and to Mary, the mother of Jesus. (See: Daniel 9:20–27; Luke 1:18–19, 26–37.)

The angel Gabriel is often shown with a horn—since many people believe he'll blow the trumpet on God's day of judgment of the earth.

And that Definition Means...

ALTAR OF INCENSE

A short stand covered with gold. Sweet-smelling incense was burned on it twice a day. This altar was inside the temple, and burning incense on it symbolized believers' prayers rising to God. Zechariah was burning incense to God when the angel Gabriel appeared to him. (See: Exodus 30:1–8; Luke 1:8–11, 19; Revelation 8:3.)

Feature

MIDIANITE INVASION! TIME FOR A MIRACLE!

When the Israelites disobeyed God, God allowed the armies of Midian to invade their land. Countless raiders swept into Israel before harvest and let their livestock eat all the Israelites' crops. The Israelites fled into caves and mountains. They were starving. This went on for seven years, year after year. They were desperate! Finally, God sent an angel to a farmer named Gideon. The angel told him to raise an army and attack the Midianites. God whittled Gideon's army down from 32,000 men to a mere 300 to make sure that the Israelites understood that it would take a miracle of *God* for them to win—and they did! (See: Judges 6–7.)

THE NAME GAME!
In Gideon's day, the Midianites were ruled by four princes—Zeeb, Zebah, Zalmunna, and Oreb. Seems like names starting with *Z* were popular with Midianite princes. (See: Judges 8:3, 12.)

MIDIAN (MIDIANITES)

Places & People

Midian was a son of Abraham, and the Midianites lived in the deserts south of Israel. Moses lived in Midian for 40 years. (See: Genesis 25:1–2; Exodus 2:15–22.)

FUN FACTS!
Claudius Lysias claimed that he'd rescued Paul from a mob when he learned that Paul was a Roman citizen. What a lie. He only found out Paul was a Roman when he was about to torture him. (Compare Acts 21:31–40; 22:24–29 with 23:26–27).

Five Times God and Angels Appeared on Earth as Men

1. The Lord and two angels appeared as men to Abraham.
2. Jacob wrestled with a "man" who was actually God.
3. The angel of the Lord appeared to Gideon.
4. The angel of the Lord appeared to Manoah once and his wife twice.
5. Two "men" (angels) talked to the women at Jesus' tomb.

(See: Genesis 18:1–2; 19:1; 32:22–30; Judges 6:11–22; 13:2–21; Luke 24:1–6.)

I Love Lists!

Four Things the Israelites Burned as Fuel

1. Wood, mostly dry sticks
2. Thornbushes, because there were so many of them
3. Dried cow poop
4. Shields, bows, arrows, war clubs, and spears

(See: Numbers 15:32; 1 Kings 17:10–12; Ecclesiastes 7:6; Ezekiel 4:15; 39:9.)

Who's that?

GAMALIEL

A highly respected Jewish rabbi. Gamaliel taught Paul when Paul was young and prevented the Sanhedrin (ruling Jewish council) from killing the apostles. (See: Acts 5:33–40; 22:3.)

GEDALIAH

A friend of the prophet Jeremiah. After the Babylonians conquered Judah, they appointed Gedaliah governor. He was killed because he trusted people too much. (See: Jeremiah 40:1–41:3.)

GEHAZI

The servant of the prophet Elisha. At first, Gehazi was a faithful servant, but later he was cursed with leprosy for being greedy. (See: 2 Kings 4:8–37; 5:20–27; 8:4–6.)

FUN FACTS!
Gehazi once asked a mom, "Is your child all right?" (2 Kings 4:26 NIV). She answered, "Everything is all right" (2 Kings 4:26 NIV). Everything *wasn't* all right, however. Her son had just died.

FUN FACTS!
When the olives were ripe, Israelite farmers beat the branches of the trees with sticks to make the olives fall. There were always some olives on the top branches that wouldn't fall. (See: Isaiah 17:6.)

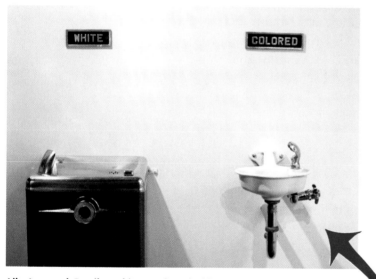

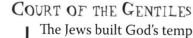

Like Jews and Gentiles, white people and African-Americans were once separated by custom—even being forced to use different drinking fountains.

And that Definition Means...

COURT OF THE GENTILES

The Jews built God's temple to worship God in, and Gentiles (non-Jews) were not allowed in it. God knew that people from every nation would be drawn to Him, however, so the Jews allowed the Gentiles to enter the courtyard just outside the temple (Revelation 11:2 KJV). This was called the Court of the Gentiles. (See: Isaiah 56:7; Acts 21:28.)

Feature

JOTHAM'S FABLE

The people of Shechem wanted Gideon to rule over them, but he refused. Then they wanted Gideon's worthless son Abimelech for their king, so he killed all of his 70 brothers. Only Jotham escaped. Abimelech then went to Shechem to be crowned. Jotham had a dangerous message, so he stood atop a nearby hill and shouted it out as a story—a fable about how the trees wanted a king, but the olive tree refused. The fig tree refused. Even the grape vine refused. Only the worthless, ground-crawling, prickly thornbush accepted. (The thornbush was Abimelech.) Then Jotham basically said, "May Abimelech destroy you, and may you destroy Abimelech!" And that's what happened. (See: Judges 8:22–23; 9:1–21, 56–57.)

FUN FACTS!
Gideon was fighting to save Israel, but the elders of Succoth mocked him and refused to give his army food. After the battle, Gideon whipped the elders with thorns and briars. (See: Judges 8:4–16.)

Six Deaths That Were Barely Avoided

1. Nabal and his farm workers barely avoided being killed.
2. Jeremiah's friends talked his enemies out of killing him.
3. Ten men avoided being killed and thrown in a water pit.
4. Joseph, Mary, and Jesus fled Bethlehem just in time.
5. Jesus escaped before He could be thrown down a cliff.
6. Paul escaped death in Damascus through an opening in the wall.

(See: 1 Samuel 25:1–34; Jeremiah 26:7–24; 41:4–8; Matthew 2:13–16; Luke 4:28–30; Acts 9:23–25.)

I Love Lists!

DAMASCUS

Damascus was a very important, ancient city in Syria. One time the apostle Paul escaped the city by being lowered in a basket through an opening in the wall. (See: Acts 9:19–25.)

Places & People

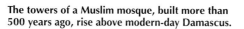

The towers of a Muslim mosque, built more than 500 years ago, rise above modern-day Damascus.

Who's that?

GIDEON

The son of a wealthy Israelite farmer who lived in Gilead. Gideon doubted that God would use him to win a war and asked God for many signs. God then used Gideon to win an amazing battle. (See: Judges 6–7.)

STRANGE BUT TRUE!
In Gideon's day, 9,700 soldiers stuck their faces down in the water and lapped like a dog when they were thirsty. They were kicked out of the army as a result. (See: Judges 7:2–8.)

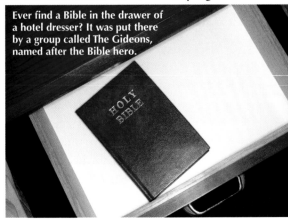
Ever find a Bible in the drawer of a hotel dresser? It was put there by a group called The Gideons, named after the Bible hero.

GOD THE FATHER

The first person in the Trinity. The other persons are God the Son (Jesus) and God the Holy Spirit. Jesus called God His Father. (See: Trinity, page 68; see also: John 14:7–11; 20:17)

FUN FACTS!
God poked fun at Israelites who burned part of a block of wood to roast meat and bake bread, then carved an idol out of the leftover wood and bowed down to it. (See: Isaiah 44:9–20.)

GOLIATH

A giant who lived in the Philistine city of Gath. Goliath was over nine feet tall. He challenged the Israelites to send a warrior to fight him, so David fought and killed him. (See: 1 Samuel 17.)

And that Definition Means...

ABBA

An Aramaic word meaning "daddy." (Aramaic is the language that Jesus and His disciples spoke.) Before He was crucified, Jesus prayed in the Garden of Gethsemane, crying out to God, "Abba, Father." The apostle Paul used the word *Abba*, too, saying that we are children of God and that we should address Him as our Father. (See: Mark 14:36; Romans 8:14–15; Galatians 4:6.)

David's slingshot knocked Goliath down. . .but the teenager used the giant's own sword to cut off Goliath's head!

ELDERS

In the Bible, elders means a council of older, wise people—usually men—chosen to rule. In Old Testament times, elders were older men who ruled a town or city in Israel. Gideon once whipped 77 elders of Succoth for not giving bread to his exhausted troops. Elders also helped rule all Israel. In New Testament times, elders were wise, mature men who were chosen to rule the individual churches. (See: Numbers 11:16–17; Judges 8:4–16; Titus 1:5–6.)

Feature

OUTLAW BECOMES GENERAL

Gilead, chief of the land of Gilead, had a wife and several sons, but he also had a son, Jephthah, by another, bad woman. When Gilead died his sons chased Jephthah away, saying, "You're not going to get any of the inheritance!" The elders of the land agreed, so Jephthah went to the land of Tob. There he became a mighty warrior and the leader of a band of adventurers. Later when the land of Gilead was overrun by enemies, the elders had to humble themselves—oh, how embarrassing!—and ask Jephthah to lead their armies. After defeating the enemy, Jephthah ruled Gilead for six years. (See: Judges 11:1–11, 32–33; 12:7.)

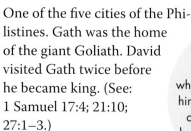

Places & People

GATH

One of the five cities of the Philistines. Gath was the home of the giant Goliath. David visited Gath twice before he became king. (See: 1 Samuel 17:4; 21:10; 27:1–3.)

Eight Times the Israelites Vanquished Giants

1. The Israelites defeated the giants Ahiman, Sheshai, and Talmai.
2. The Israelites killed monstrous Og.
3. David killed the giant Goliath.
4. Abishai, David's nephew, killed the giant Ishbi-Benob.
5. Sibbecai the Israelite killed the giant Saph.
6–7. Elhanan from Bethlehem killed Goliath Junior and also killed Lahmi, Goliath's brother.
8. Jonathan, David's nephew, killed a multi-fingered, multi-toed giant.

(See: Numbers 13:22; 21:32–35; Deuteronomy 3:3–11; Judges 1:10; 1 Samuel 17; 2 Samuel 21:15–21; 1 Chronicles 20:5.)

I Love Lists!

STRANGE BUT TRUE!
David visited Gath, and when the Philistines recognized him, he pretended that he was crazy. David drooled in his beard and scratched the door like a dog. (See: 1 Samuel 21:10–15.)

Who's that?

HABAKKUK

A prophet when the Babylonians were about to conquer Judah. Habakkuk first asked God why He didn't punish evildoers—then asked why He used the Babylonians to punish them. (See: Habakkuk 1.)

HAGAR

Sarah's Egyptian slave. Sarah thought she couldn't have children, so she gave Hagar to Abraham as a concubine (lesser wife). Hagar bore Abraham a son named Ishmael. (See: Genesis 16.)

HAGGAI

A prophet who lived after the Jews returned from Babylon. God's temple had been destroyed, so Haggai and another prophet named Zechariah encouraged the Jews to rebuild it. (See: Haggai 1:1–12; Ezra 5:1–2; 6:14.)

FUN FACTS!
Habakkuk said that when the Red Sea came crashing down, drowning Pharaoh's chariots and horses, God was trampling the sea with *His* chariots and horses. (See: Habakkuk 3:8, 15.)

FUN FACTS!
Hagar wasn't *really* a big lady, but Paul compared her to a mountain. In Galatians 4:25, Paul said that Hagar was like Mount Sinai, where God gave Moses the Law.

And that Definition Means...

DEDICATE

To set something apart for a special use. "To dedicate" is sometimes called "to consecrate," especially if a ceremony goes along with it. God told the Israelites to dedicate their firstborn sons to Him. We are to dedicate our lives to God. Romans 12:1 (KJV) talks about offering our bodies as a "living sacrifice" to God. (See Sanctify, page 144; see also: Exodus 13:1–2.)

OFFERING

The Law of Moses told the Jews to offer (give) God offerings. This could mean offering bread to God. Often, however, an offering meant a lamb or goat or some other animal that was sacrificed (killed) on the altar. Sometimes God commanded the Israelites to give an offering of gold and other valuables. (See: Exodus 25:1–7; Leviticus 1:2–5; 7:11–12.)

FUN FACTS!
Abraham once stood guard over the dead bodies of animals he'd sacrificed and drove off the vultures and other birds of prey that swooped down to eat them. (See: Genesis 15:9–11.)

Feature

SAMSON'S FANTASTIC FOX-FIRE FEAT

A Philistine father once made Samson furious by giving away Samson's bride to another man. In retaliation, Samson went out, caught 300 foxes, and tied them tail to tail in pairs. He then attached a torch to every pair of tails and set the foxes loose. The freaked-out, fearful foxes fled like fiends trying to flee the fiery torches—with both foxes in each pair trying to run different directions! With 150 fox-teams running wild, they burned down miles of Philistine fields and vineyards and olive groves. Now think how much *work* that was to catch those 300 foxes in the first place. You try catching just *one*! (See: Judges 15:1–5.)

A typical North American red fox.

Five Water Discoveries in the Desert

1. Hagar, dying of thirst, discovered a well in the desert.
2. Anah found hot springs in the desert while grazing donkeys.
3. God brought water out of a rock at Massah for Moses and the thirsty Israelites.
4. At Kadesh, using Moses, God once again brought water from a rock.
5. God caused water to spring out of the ground for Samson.

(See: Genesis 21:15–19; 36:24; Exodus 17:1–7; Numbers 20:1–11; Judges 15:16–19.)

I Love Lists!

STRANGE BUT TRUE!
Freedom for a tooth! In Israel, if you were a slave but your master hit you and knocked out a tooth, you got to go free for that missing tooth! (See: Exodus 21:26–27.)

Who's that?

HAM

The youngest of Noah's three sons. Ham was the father of the Egyptians and other African peoples. Noah cursed Ham's son, Canaan. (See: Genesis 9:18–25; 10:6–20.)

HAMAN

A powerful man in Persia and an enemy of the Jews. Haman persuaded the Persian king to make a law to kill all the Jews, but the Jews were spared and Haman was killed instead. (See: Esther 3; 7.)

THE NAME GAME!
Aspatha means "horse-given." Now, what kind of father would call his son "horse-given"? Well, Haman, one of the greatest villains in the Bible, that's who. (See: Esther 9:6–10.)

HANNAH

The mother of Samuel. She promised God that if He gave her a son, she'd give the child back to Him. When Samuel was still a boy, Hannah took him to live at the Tent of Meeting. (See: 1 Samuel 1.)

And that Definition Means...

TENT OF MEETING

The "Tent of Meeting" (Exodus 29:42 NIV) was also called the "tabernacle" in the King James Bible. When the Israelites were wandering in the desert, they needed a place to keep the Ark of the Covenant and other holy objects. They also needed a place to worship God. God instructed Moses to build a large tent where He could meet with them. This tent had a large fence made of cloth around it. (See: Exodus 26.)

FUN FACTS!
Talk about an unexpected job! The Israelites, led by Moses, headed off to Canaan to become farmers, but they first spent 40 years as shepherds in the desert. (See: Numbers 14:33.)

A model of the ancient tabernacle, set up in modern-day Israel.

Feature

THE TRIBE OF DAN MIGRATES NORTH

After much of Canaan had been conquered, Joshua divided the land between the tribes of Israel and told them to settle down. It was then up to each tribe to conquer the Canaanites remaining in its territory. The members of the tribe of Dan had a problem, however. The best land in their area was controlled by strong Amorite and Philistine armies, and the Danites were stuck up in the hills. As their population increased, they felt squeezed, so they sent out five spies. The spies found good, undefended land far to the north, so the Danites marched there, attacked the Canaanites, and won. Finally they had enough room to settle down. (See: Judges 1:34; 18:1–31.)

Crazy Stuff That Happened in Vineyards

1. Noah planted a vineyard, grew grapes, made wine, and got drunk.
2. Once 200 warriors hid in a vineyard, jumped out, and grabbed 200 dancing girls.
3. Elijah confronted King Ahab in Naboth's vineyard.
4. A farmer's lazy son finally decided to work in the vineyard.
5. Wicked workers killed the vineyard owner's servants and son.

(See: Genesis 9:20–21; Judges 20:47; 21:12–23; 1 Kings 21:17–24; Matthew 21:28–31, 33–41

I love Lists!

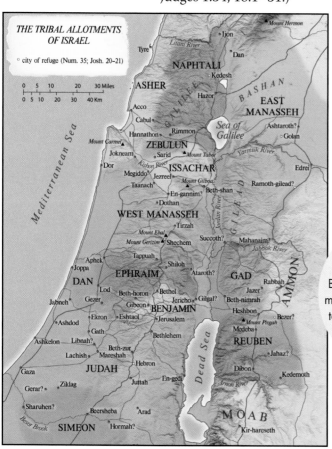

THE TRIBAL ALLOTMENTS OF ISRAEL

° city of refuge (Num. 35; Josh. 20–21)

0   5   10   20   30 Miles
0 5 10   20   30   40 Km

Mediterranean Sea

Mount Hermon

Ijon

Tyre
Litani River
Dan

NAPHTALI
Kedesh

ASHER
Hazor
B A S H A N

Acco
Cabul
Hannathon   Rimmon
Sea of Galilee
EAST MANASSEH
Ashtaroth?
Golan

Mount Carmel
ZEBULUN
Jokneam   Sarid   Mount Tabor
Kishon River
Yarmuk River

Dor
Megiddo   Jezreel   ISSACHAR
Taanach   Mount Gilboa
Edrei

En-gannim?
Beth-shan
Ramoth-gilead

Dothan
G I L E A D

WEST MANASSEH
Tirzah

Mount Ebal
Mount Gerizim   Shechem
Succoth?
Mahanaim?
Jabbok River

Tappuah
Shiloh

Aphek
Joppa
EPHRAIM
Ataroth?
GAD
Jazer
Rabbah

DAN
Lod   Beth-horon   Bethel
Jericho?   Gilgal?
Beth-nimrah

Jabneh
Gezer
Gibeon   BENJAMIN
Heshbon
Bezer?

Ekron   Eshtaol
Jerusalem
Mount Pisgah
Medeba?

Ashdod
Gath
Bethlehem
REUBEN

Ashkelon   Libnah?
Beth-zur
Jahaz?

Lachish   Mareshah
Hebron
Dibon

Gaza
JUDAH
En-gedi
Kedemoth

Ziklag
Juttah
Arnon River

Gerar?
M O A B

Sharuhen?
Beersheba   Arad

Besor Brook
SIMEON   Hormah?
Kir-hareseth

Dead Sea

A M M O N

FUN FACTS!
Dan was the northernmost town in Israel, and Beersheba was the southernmost, so when people wanted to say "all Israel," they said, "from Dan to Beersheba" (2 Samuel 17:11 NKJV).

FUN FACTS!
When Israelite farmers harvested their grain and ground it into flour, the very first thing they baked—a cake—had to be given to God. (See: Numbers 15:18–21.)

HEROD THE GREAT

An Edomite who became king of Judea in the days of the Romans. He rebuilt the Jewish temple but was a cruel, suspicious king. He tried to kill Baby Jesus. (See: Matthew 2:1–16.)

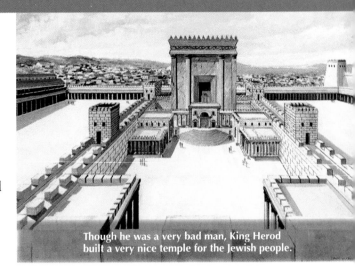

Though he was a very bad man, King Herod built a very nice temple for the Jewish people.

HEROD AGRIPPA

A grandson of Herod the Great. He was the King Herod who killed James, John's brother. He loved it when the crowds said he had "the voice of a god" (Acts 12:22 NIV), so God let him be eaten by worms and die. (See: Acts 12:1–4, 19–23.)

THE NAME GAME!
Herod Agrippa had a servant named "Blastus" (Acts 12:20). *Blastus* doesn't mean "please shoot us with a ray gun." It means "bud." More guys get called Bud than Blastus these days.

HEROD ANTIPAS

A son of Herod the Great. When John the Baptist criticized him for marrying his brother's wife, this Herod put John in prison. He then be-headed John and had his head brought back out on a platter. Later, he and his soldiers mocked Jesus. (See: Mark 6:17–29; Luke 23:6–12.)

DISCIPLE

A follower of a teacher, such as the disciples of John the Baptist. Usually in the New Testament, however, *disciple* refers to the followers of Jesus. Jesus' followers were not called "Christians" until later on. Jesus said that to truly be His disciples, we have to obey His teachings. He also said that His disciples would be known by their love for others. (See: Matthew 9:14; John 8:31; 13:35; Acts 6:7; 11:26.)

Feature

GOD'S ARK PLAGUES THE PHILISTINES

The Ark of the Covenant was a gold-covered chest that symbolized the presence of God, so one day the Israelites carried it into battle, hoping it would help them win. Instead, the Philistines won the battle, captured the Ark, and took it to the city of Ashdod. Soon a plague hit Ashdod and people started getting tumors (painful swellings). Quickly the Philistines of Ashdod sent the Ark to Gath. Everyone there was struck with tumors, too, and panicked. They tried taking the Ark to Ekron, but the men of Ekron stopped them. They told their rulers to send the Ark back to the Israelites, loaded down with offerings of golden rats and models of tumors—so they did. (See: 1 Samuel 5:1–6:14.)

A rock badger looks out from his stony home.

Five Rodents Registered in the Writings

1. Bats—God told the Israelites not to eat bats.
2. Rats—the Philistines made small golden rats.
3. Rock badgers (coneys)—these rodents live in the rocks.
4. Moles—the wicked will throw their golden idols to the "moles" (Isaiah 2:20 KJV).
5. Mice—some Israelites cooked mice and ate them.

(See: Leviticus 11:13, 19; 1 Samuel 6:5; Proverbs 30:26; Isaiah 66:17.)

I Love Lists!

THE NAME GAME!

Esau had a funny nickname: *Red.* (*Edom* is Hebrew for "red.") He was called this after he traded his birthright for a stew made of red lentils. (See: Genesis 25:30.)

FUN FACTS!

James and John were brothers. James was the *first* of the apostles to die, and John was the *last* apostle to die. He lived longer than any of the other 12 apostles. (See: Acts 12:1–2.)

Who's that?

HEZEKIAH

A good king of Judah during the days of the Assyrian empire. When the Assyrians mocked God, Hezekiah prayed, and God sent an angel to wipe out the Assyrian army. (See: 2 Kings 18–19.)

HIRAM

The king of Tyre in the days of David and Solomon. Hiram sent workers and materials to David to build his palace, and later to Solomon to build God's temple. (See: 2 Samuel 5:11; 1 Kings 5; 7:13–15.)

HULDAH

A prophetess during the days of King Josiah. When the long-lost Book of the Law was found in the temple, Huldah gave tenderhearted Josiah a comforting prophecy. (See: 2 Kings 22:3–20.)

An Assyrian Archer

STRANGE BUT TRUE!
When King Hezekiah was dying of a huge boil, God told the prophet Isaiah to put a poultice (a veggie pack) of mashed-up figs on his boil—and it cured him. (See: Isaiah 38:1–5, 21.)

And that Definition Means...

LAW, THE

The Law of Moses, the first five books of the Bible—Genesis, Exodus, Leviticus, Numbers, and Deuteronomy. God gave Moses the Law on Mount Sinai and commanded His people to obey it. The Jews called all the other books of scripture "the Prophets," and they called the entire Old Testament "the prophets and the law" (Matthew 11:13 KJV). (See also: Luke 24:44.)

SCRIPTURES

Scriptures means "the Writings"—the holy Writings that God gave to His people. For the Jews and the early Christians, the scriptures meant the Law and the Prophets in the Old Testament. After a while, however, Christians realized that the writings of Paul and the other apostles were *also* scripture, along with "the rest of the Scriptures" (2 Peter 3:15–16 NKJV). (See also: Luke 24:27.)

Feature

GOD GIVES THE ISRAELITES A KING

For hundreds of years Israel had no king except for God, and God used judges—wise, courageous men like the prophet Samuel—to lead them. But when Nahash, king of the Ammonites, began attacking, the Israelites were desperate for a king to lead them into battle. What they were asking for was wrong, but God had mercy and told Samuel, "Listen to them and give them a king" (1 Samuel 8:22 NIV). Just the same, after Saul was proclaimed king in a big celebration, God sent a heavy rain to ruin their crops. The people were sorry, but they had a king now, so Samuel told them *and* their king to follow God. (See: 1 Samuel 8:1–22; 11:14–15; 12:12–22.)

Five Bible Characters with the Same Name

1. A male Noah and a female Noah
2. A good Jonathan and a bad Jonathan
3. A bad Saul and a good Saul
4. A bad Judas and a good Judas
5. A bad Ananias and a good Ananias

(See: Genesis 6:9; Numbers 26:33; Judges 18:30; 1 Samuel 14:1; 16:1; Matthew 26: 14–15; Acts 5: 1–5; 9:10–20; 15:22.)

I Love Lists!

FUN FACTS!
When King David bought a hill, he paid 15 pounds of gold for it. When King Omri bought a hill some years later, he paid 150 pounds of silver for it. (See: 1 Kings 16:24; 1 Chronicles 21:25.)

FUN FACTS!
In Solomon's day, one shiny new chariot from Egypt cost 15 pounds of silver. Expensive! You could buy four Egyptian horses for that same price! (See: 1 Kings 10:29.)

A modern model of an ancient Roman chariot.

Who's that?

HOLY SPIRIT

The third person of the Trinity, also called the Spirit of God and the Comforter. Jesus promised to send the Spirit to live in the hearts of believers. (See: Trinity—below; see also: John 14:25–26; 16:5–14.)

FUN FACTS!
The Holy Spirit told an old prophet named Simeon that he wouldn't die before he saw the Savior of Israel—and sure enough, Simeon lived to see baby Jesus! (Luke 2:25–32).

HOSEA

A prophet of the northern kingdom of Israel. Hosea had a very unfaithful wife. Israel was rich and prosperous at this time, but Hosea rebuked it for turning from God. (See: Hosea 3–4.)

ISAAC

The son of Abraham and Sarah. Isaac was born by a miracle when his parents were both old. When Isaac was young, Abraham nearly sacrificed him on an altar. (See: Genesis 21:1–7; 22:1–14.)

FUN FACTS!
When they were old, both Isaac and Ahijah became blind. People tried to trick both of them. Isaac fell for it, but Ahijah wasn't fooled at all. (See: Genesis 27:1–29; 1 Kings 14:1–6.)

And that Definition Means...

DISCIPLINE

Also called chastisement. In the Bible, discipline is not just punishment for breaking rules, but an important part of training to help us grow up to become mature, obedient Christians. Hebrews 12:4–13 gives an excellent explanation of God's discipline: "God disciplines us for our good, that we may share in his holiness" (Hebrews 12:10 NIV).

TRINITY

There is one God, but He exists in a *trinity* (three persons)—the Father, the Son, and the Holy Spirit. The Holy Spirit is one with God because He is God's very own spirit, and Jesus is also one with His Father. When Jesus was baptized, the Son was present, the Father spoke from heaven, and the Spirit descended. All three members of the Trinity were there. (See: Matthew 3:16–17; John 10:30; 1 Corinthians 2:10–11.)

A young boy acts out the story of William Tell—an expert Swiss archer forced to shoot an apple off his son's head.

Feature

DEATH PENALTY FOR EATING HONEY

Prince Jonathan had just won a battle, and the Philistines were now fleeing. Then King Saul did something dumb. He basically said, "Cursed be any man who eats food today before we beat the Philistines!" Soon the Israelites began getting weak as they chased the Philistines. Jonathan hadn't heard his father, so when he passed a beehive he grabbed some honey and ate it. Saul was so furious that he wanted to kill his own son—all for eating a little honey! Fortunately the Israelites stood up for Jonathan and talked Saul out of killing him. (See: 1 Samuel 14:1–46.)

FUN FACTS!
Ancient warriors used to go into battle all decked out in gold jewelry. The problem was, if the *other* army won and you were dead, the enemy got to take all your loot. (See: Judges 8:24–26.)

Five Famous Archers

1. Ishmael, the son of Abraham, was an archer in the desert.
2. Jonathan, David's friend, was a famous archer.
3. An Aramean soldier killed King Ahab with a fluke arrow.
4. The prophet Elisha and the king of Israel shot a bow together.
5. The men of Lydia were "famous as archers" (Isaiah 66:19 NIV).

(See: Genesis 21:20; 2 Samuel 1:17–18, 22; 1 Kings 22:29–40; 2 Kings 13:15–17.)

I love Lists!

Five Prophets with No Names

1. The man of God from Judah
2. An old prophet
3. The prophet who spoke to King Ahab
4. The "strike me" prophet
5. The prophet who rebuked King Amaziah

(See: 1 Kings 13:1, 11, 20, 27; 20:13, 22, 28, 35, 37, 41; 2 Chronicles 25:14–15.)

Who's that?

ISAIAH

A great prophet of Judah in the days of King Hezekiah and the Assyrian empire. Isaiah gave several amazing prophecies about the coming Messiah, Jesus. (See: Isaiah 7:14; 9:6–7; 53.)

REALLY GROSS!
The Lord describes things in a funny way at times. Speaking through Isaiah, God said He would make the Egyptians so dizzy they would be like a drunk man staggering around in his own vomit. (See: Isaiah 19:14.)

ISHMAEL

The son of Hagar, Sarah's Egyptian servant. Ishmael's father was Abraham. Ishmael was mean to young Isaac, so Abraham sent Ishmael and Hagar away. (See: Genesis 16; 21:8–21.)

JACOB

Twin brother of Esau. Jacob deceived his father, Isaac, to get Esau's blessing. Jacob's name was later changed to Israel, and his 12 sons were the ancestors of the 12 tribes of Israel. (See: Genesis 27:1–29; 32:28; 35:22–26.)

FUN FACTS!
When Jacob met his brother Esau many years after cheating him, Jacob gave Esau a huge present: 220 goats, 220 sheep, 50 cattle, 30 camels, and 30 donkeys. (See: Genesis 32:13–15.)

FUN FACTS!
When Jacob wanted to convince his blind father that he was Esau, Jacob wore one of Esau's robes. When Isaac caught the—ahem!—*smell* of Esau's clothes, he was convinced. (See: Genesis 27:15, 26–27.)

A camel rests in the deserts of India.

FUN FACTS!
What happened to all Jacob's camels? He had many camels when he entered Canaan, but some 20 years later, all his sons had to carry grain on was donkeys. (See: Genesis 32:7; 42:26.)

And that Definition Means...

MESSIAH

The Hebrew word *Messiah* means "anointed one," and the Greek word *Christ* also means "anointed one." When Jesus is called Jesus the Christ it means Jesus the Messiah. In Jesus' day, many Israelites were waiting for the Messiah, the anointed King, to arrive and bring truth and justice. They believed that the Messiah would be the Son of God. (See: John 1:41, 49; 4:25–26.)

Feature

MUSICIAN ESCAPES OUT WINDOW

When David was a young man, he married King Saul's daughter Michal. Now, one afternoon while David was playing his harp for the king, an evil spirit possessed Saul, and he tried to impale David with a spear. David escaped to his house, but Michal knew that her dad had gone berserk and that he wouldn't stop till David was dead. She urged David to escape out the window that night, then she put a dummy in his bed, covered it with clothes, and put goat's hair at its head. When Saul sent some men the next morning to arrest David, there was the dummy—but David was long gone. (See: 1 Samuel 19:9–16.)

Places & People

ISRAEL (ISRAELITES)

God changed Jacob's name to *Israel*—which means "ruling with God." When Israel's descendants, the children of Israel (or Israelites), conquered Canaan, they renamed the land Israel. (See: Genesis 32:28.)

Six kids make up a big family today—but that's nothing compared to some of the Bible's families!

Five Men with Way, Way Too Many Wives, Listed from the Most to the Least

1. Solomon had 700 wives and 300 concubines (lesser wives).
2. Rehoboam had 18 wives and 60 concubines.
3. David had at least 6 wives and 10 concubines.
4. Abijah had 14 wives.
5. Gideon (Jerub-Baal) had "many wives" (Judges 8:30 RSV).

(see: 2 Samuel 3:2–5; 15:16; 1 Kings 11:3; 2 Chronicles 11:21; 13:21.)

I Love Lists!

Seven Bible Records for the Most Children, Listed from the Most to the Least

1. Rehoboam had 28 sons and 60 daughters.
2. Gideon (also called Jerub-Baal) had 70 sons.
3. Ahab had 70 sons.
4. Abijah had 22 sons and 16 daughters.
5. Jair had 30 sons.
6. Heman had 14 sons and three daughters.
7. Jacob had 12 sons and at least two daughters

(See: Genesis 35:22–26; Judges 8:30; 2 Kings 10:1; 1 Chronicles 25:5; 2 Chronicles 11:21; 13:21.)

Who's that?

JABIN

Two Canaanite kings were named Jabin. Joshua defeated the first Jabin, and many years later Deborah and Barak defeated the second one. (See: Joshua 11:1–10; Judges 4.)

JAEL

Heber the Kenite was friends with Jabin, but his wife Jael was on Israel's side—so when Jabin's general, Sisera, fled a battle and hid in Jael's tent, Jael killed him. (See: Judges 4:11–22; 5:24–27.)

Sisera "gets nailed" by Jael in this painting from the 1700s.

AWESOME FEAT!
The Canaanite general Sisera was killed by a woman. When he fled from a battle, hid in Jael's tent, then fell asleep, she hammered a tent peg through his head! (See: Judges 4:17–21.)

JAIRUS

The leader of a Jewish synagogue. His 12-year-old daughter died, but when Jesus came, after crossing Lake Gennesaret, He sent away the mourners and raised Jairus's daughter from the dead. (See: Mark 5:22–43.)

STRANGE BUT TRUE!
In Israel, when someone in a wealthy family died, like Jairus's daughter, often the families hired a "noisy crowd" (Matthew 9:23 NIV) of strangers called "wailing women" (Jeremiah 9:17 NIV) to come in and cry.

And that Definition Means...

FORGIVENESS

Also called "pardon" and "remission of sins." To forgive someone who has wronged you means giving up your claim for repayment or revenge. Forgiveness also means letting go of grudges against others. When we repent of our sins, God forgives us. Jesus said that we should forgive others, just as God has forgiven us. (See: Matthew 18:21–35; Acts 2:38; Colossians 3:12–13.)

FUN FACTS!
In Joshua's day, Piram was an Amorite king who attacked Gibeon, Israel's ally. You get an idea of the kind of person Piram was by his name. It means "wild donkey." (See: Joshua 10:3.)

Feature

ABIGAIL SAVES THE FOOL AND THE FARM

Once a beautiful woman named Abigail was married to a pigheaded man named Nabal. (*Nabal* means "fool.") Nabal had 3,000 sheep, and when he sheared them to sell his wool, he threw a big feast. Now, for months David and his men had helped watch over Nabal's flocks, so now David asked if Nabal could spare anything from his feast. Instead of showing gratitude, Nabal hurled insults at David. Unfortunately, David decided to take revenge, but as his men were coming to wipe out Nabal and his hired hands, Abigail heard what had happened and quickly sent David a ton of food. Nabal died of a heart attack about 11 days later, and Abigail and David were married. (See: 1 Samuel 25.)

Places & People

GALILEE, SEA OF

This small lake, also called Lake Gennesaret, is in north Israel. Four of Jesus' disciples were fishermen there, and Jesus often preached near it. (See: Mark 1:16–20; Luke 5:1–2.)

Fishing boats along the shore of the Sea of Galilee.

Eight People Who Came Back from the Dead

1. The widow of Zarephath's son
2. The Shunammite woman's son
3. A dead man touched by Elisha's bones (You gotta read this story found in 2 Kings 13:20–21!)
4. Jesus, the most important one of all—because His resurrection powers our own!
5. Jairus's daughter
6. Lazarus
7. Dorcas, also called Tabitha
8. Eutychus

(See: 1 Kings 17:10, 17–24; 2 Kings 4:8–37; 13:20–21; Matthew 28; Mark 5:21–43; 16; Luke 24; John 11:1–44; 20; Acts 9:36–43; 20:7–12.)

I love Lists!

Six Things Israelites Did when They Heard Terrible News

1. Sprinkled dirt or ashes on their heads
2. Tore their clothing
3. Pulled out hair from their head and beard
4. Fasted from food and water
5. Dressed in rough, itchy sackcloth
6. Covered their heads

(See: Joshua 7:6; Ezra 9:3, 5; 10:6; Isaiah 22:12; Jeremiah 14:3.)

Who's that?

JAMES

One of Jesus' 12 apostles. Jesus called him and his brother, John, the "Sons of Thunder." James, the first apostle to die, was killed by King Herod Agrippa. (See: Mark 1:19–20; 3:17; Acts 12:1–2.)

JAMES

One of Jesus' younger brothers. At first, James didn't believe in Jesus. Later, James became the head of the church in Jerusalem. (See: Matthew 13:55; John 7:5; Acts 21:18.)

IMPORTANT IDEA!
One day Jesus is going to get married! Symbolically, that is. He will marry the Church, which is called the Bride of Christ. (See: Revelation 19:7–9; 2 Corinthians 11:2.)

James and John wade ashore to follow Jesus in this painting from the 1880s.

JAPHETH

One of the three sons of Noah. Japheth was the ancestor of the Europeans—from the Russians of the north to the Greeks in the islands of the south. (See: Genesis 10:1–5.)

And that Definition Means...

REBUKE

To give a stern talk to someone, to give him or her a harsh lecture. The prophet Samuel gave King Saul a very stiff rebuke. Paul said that sometimes it's necessary to rebuke people, but that a young man should not harshly rebuke an older man; instead, he should explain things gently to him. (See: 1 Samuel 15:16–19; 1 Timothy 5:1; Titus 1:13.)

Feature

A GHOST STORY

Even though King Saul himself had outlawed mediums, when he wanted to know how a battle against the Philistines would go—and God was no longer talking to him—Saul went to a medium at Endor one night. He asked the hag to bring up the spirit of the dead prophet Samuel. Of course, the "witch of Endor" couldn't summon godly Samuel, but God permitted the prophet to appear—scaring the medium out of her wits! Samuel then gave bad news to Saul: "Tomorrow you and your sons will be with me" (1 Samuel 28:19 NIV)—meaning they'd be *dead*! Sure enough, Saul and his three sons died on the battlefield the next day. (See: 1 Samuel 28, 31.)

FUN FACTS!
In Israel, shields were made of wood covered with leather. To make swords bounce off their shields, men rubbed olive oil on them. (See: 2 Samuel 1:21.)

Places & People

GREECE (GREEKS)

Greece was—and still is—a country in southern Europe. Greece once had an empire that ruled much of the Middle East. In Jesus' day, Greece was just a province of the Roman Empire.

IMPORTANT IDEA!

If we want to serve God, we need to wear armor and helmets, carry a shield, and bear a sword. All of this is *spiritual* armor, of course! Read about it in Ephesians 6:11–17.

Suits of armor like this one protected soldiers centuries ago.

Seven Prophets Who Scolded Rulers

1. Samuel rebuked King Saul.
2. Nathan rebuked King David.
3. Ahijah rebuked King Jeroboam and his wife.
4. Jehu rebuked King Baasha.
5. Elijah rebuked King Ahab.
6. Micaiah rebuked King Ahab.
7. John the Baptist rebuked King Herod Antipas.

(See: 1 Samuel 13:11–14; 15:13–23; 2 Samuel 12:1–12; 1 Kings 14:1–14; 16:1–4; 17:1; 21:17–26; 22:15–28; Mark 6:17–20.)

Eight Famous Female Followers of Jesus

1. Zebedee's wife, the mother of James and John
2. Mary Magdalene
3. Mary, the mother of James and Joses
4. Salome
5. Joanna the wife of Cuza, King Herod Antipas's steward
6. Susanna
7–8. Mary and Martha, the sisters of Lazarus

(See: Matthew 20:20; 27:55–56; Mark 16:1; Luke 8:2–3; 10:38–39; 24:9–10; John 11:1–3.)

Who's that?

JEHOAHAZ

The son of Jehu, king of Israel. Because of his sins, God let the Arameans completely overrun Israel, but King Jehoahaz cried out to God, and the Arameans were defeated. (See: 2 Kings 13:1–9.)

JEHOIACHIN

One of the last kings of Judah. Jehoiachin (also called Jeconiah) ruled only three months, but the line of David—including Jesus—descends from him. (See: 2 Kings 24:8–16; 25:27–30; Matthew 1:12–16.)

FUN FACTS!
Shebna carved out a fancy tomb for himself among the kings of Judah—without permission. God said that he'd throw Shebna like a ball into a faraway country. (See: Isaiah 22:15–18.)

JEHOIADA

A high priest. Jehoiada hid baby Joash in God's temple for years. When Joash was seven, Jehoiada gathered a small army, declared Joash king, and had evil Queen Athaliah killed. (See: 2 Kings 11.)

And that Definition Means...

TEN COMMANDMENTS

When God gave Moses the Law, it contained hundreds of commandments for the Jews to obey. But God wrote the ten most important laws on two stone tablets. These laws are known as the Ten Commandments. (See: Exodus 20:1–17; 31:18.)

FUN FACTS!
Nehushta was the mother of evil King Jehoiachin. She surrendered to the Babylonians with her son, then traveled as a fellow-prisoner with him to Babylon. (See 2 Kings 24:8, 12, 15.)

FUN FACTS!
King Manasseh was so foolish that he bowed down and worshipped the stars in the sky. He even built two altars to the stars inside God's temple. (See: 2 Chronicles 33:1–5.)

Actor Charlton Heston plays Moses, holding the Ten Commandments, in a movie from 1956.

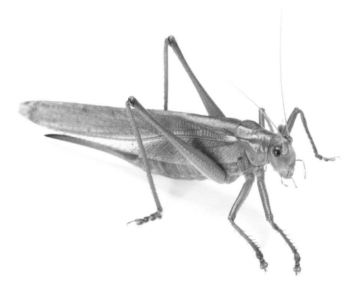

Grasshoppers are big for bugs—but compared to a person, they're tiny. That's how the Israelites felt when they saw giants in the promised land!

Five Times People Were Compared to Insects

1. The Israelites felt "like grasshoppers" (Numbers 13:33 NKJV) next to the giants.
2. David compared himself to a "flea" (1 Samuel 26:20).
3. Bildad said "man, who is but a maggot" (Job 25:6 NIV) cannot be pure in heart.
4. The psalm writer said, "I am a worm, and no man" (Psalm 22:6 RSV).
5. The psalm writer prayed for the wicked to melt like a snail (or slug) (Psalm 58:8 KJV, NIV).

I Love Lists!

Feature

GIFT-GIVING GUY BECOMES KING

David and his men had left their wives, children, and flocks in Ziklag (in Judah) to go to battle. When they returned, they found that Amalekites had raided Ziklag and taken everything. They chased the Amalekites, defeated them, and recovered everything—and then some! The Amalekites had raided many other towns in Judah and elsewhere, so David now had *huge* flocks and herds. David not only gave sheep and cattle back to the people they'd been stolen from, he sent some of the plunder as gifts to the elders of Judah. A short while later all the elders made David king of Judah. (See: 1 Samuel 30; 2 Samuel 2:1–4.)

Places & People

ARAM (ARAMEANS)

Aram was a powerful kingdom in what is now Syria, north of Israel. The Arameans fought many battles trying to conquer Israel. Naaman was an Aramean. (See: 2 Kings 5; 6:8–24; 7:5–7.)

Who's ? that?

JEHOIAKIM

The disobedient king of Judah in the days of the prophet Jeremiah. Jehoiakim refused to listen to Jeremiah and burned his scroll of prophecies. (See: Jeremiah 22:18–19; 36.)

JEHORAM

A wicked king of Judah. He married evil Athaliah, Ahab's daughter. Disaster hit Judah in Jehoram's days and he died a painful death—his bowels fell out! (See: 2 Kings 8:16–24; 2 Chronicles 21:4–20.)

JEHOSHAPHAT

A good king of Judah who won great battles. He was an ally of the evil kings of Israel, however, so God destroyed his fleet of ships. (See: 2 Chronicles 20.)

FUN FACTS!
Evil-Merodach was a Babylonian king. Despite his name, he was a *good* ruler who released Jehoiakim's son, King Jehoiachin of Judah, from prison and let him eat at his table. (See: Jeremiah 52:31–34.)

FUN FACTS!
King Solomon's trading ships brought him tons of gold from Ophir, but when King Jehoshaphat built trading ships, God wrecked them. (See: 1 Kings 9:26–28; 2 Chronicles 20:35–37.)

And that Definition Means...

HALLELUJAH, ALLELUIA

A Hebrew word that means "praise the Lord." It is often translated as "praise the Lord" or "thank the Lord," though sometimes the original word *hallelujah* is used. (See: Psalm 106:1; Revelation 19:1.)

HOSANNA

Hosanna is a Hebrew word that means, "LORD, save us!" (Psalm 118:25 NIV). It was also a shout of praise to God. When Jesus rode triumphantly into Jerusalem on a donkey, the crowds shouted, "Hosanna to the Son of David! . . . Hosanna in the highest!" (Matthew 21:6–9 NKJV).

People lay coats and tree branches before Jesus, shouting "Hosanna!" as He rides into Jerusalem.

Feature

TAKING THE ARK TO JERUSALEM

For years the Ark of the Covenant had been at a city called Baalah. When King David wanted to bring it to Jerusalem, he had it put on a cart and oxen pulled it down the road. At one point the oxen stumbled and a man named Uzzah grabbed the Ark to steady it—and was struck dead! David was so afraid that he left the Ark there. Later on, he did things the *right* way. There were gold rings on the side of the Ark for poles to fit through, and David had God's priests carry the Ark with the poles on their shoulders. On the second try he was able to bring the Ark to Jerusalem. (See: 2 Samuel 6:1–15; 1 Chronicles 15:1–15.)

Four People with Gross Diseases— REALLY GROSS!!

1. King Asa became so severely "diseased in his feet" (2 Chronicles 16:12 NKJV) that it killed him (2 Chronicles 16:11–13 NKJV).
2. Evil King Jehoram had such a horrible disease in his bowels that his bowels dropped out, killing him (2 Chronicles 21:18–19 NIV).
3. Job was attacked by Satan with "painful sores from the soles of his feet to the top of his head" (Job 2:7 NIV). "He sat in the midst of the ashes" (Job 2:8 NKJV) and scraped away the scabs and pus.
4. Proud King Herod Agrippa was "eaten by worms and died" (Acts 12:23 RSV).

I Love Lists!

THE NAME GAME!
Talk about names that sound like chickens cackling, get these: *Bakbakkar*, *Bakbuk*, and *Bakbukiah*. They mean "searcher," "bottle," and "wasted by the Lord." (See: 1 Chronicles 9:15; Ezra 2:51; Nehemiah 12:9.)

FUN FACTS!
Two evil kings, Manasseh and Amon, weren't buried in the royal tombs with the other kings of Judah. They were buried in the palace garden instead. (See: 2 Kings 21:18, 25–26.)

Who's that?

JEHU

The energetic commander of Israel's army. God made Jehu the new king, told him to kill the evil rulers (Ahaziah and Jezebel), and to wipe out Baal-worship—so Jehu did. (See: 2 Kings 9–10.)

JEREMIAH

A prophet in the final years of Judah. Jeremiah warned the people and the rulers of Judah to repent but they didn't. The lamenting Jeremiah is called the Weeping Prophet. (See: Jeremiah 1:1–10; 40:1–3.)

JEROBOAM

After King Solomon died, the northern tribes rebelled against his son, Rehoboam, and created their own nation called Israel. Jeroboam was northern Israel's first king. (See: 1 Kings 12.)

REALLY GROSS!
Rather than fight with the new king, Jehu, the elders of Samaria killed the 70 sons of the former king, descendants of Ahab, and delivered all 70 heads to Jehu in baskets. (See: 2 Kings 10:1–8.)

FUN FACTS!
The book of Jeremiah (39:10) tells us that one day some poor Israelites had nothing, and the next day they owned vineyards, houses, and fields. The former owners had been shipped off to Babylon.

And that Definition Means...

GENTILE

Anyone who is not a Jew. The Hebrew word for "nation" or "people" is *gôyim*, so when God talked about other nations or peoples, he called them gôyim, or Gentiles. Since other nations were idol-worshippers, God told the Jews to keep separate from them. Later, Christ broke down the wall between Gentiles and Jews and allowed Gentiles to be saved also. (See: Ephesians 2:11–14.)

"Gentiles" come in all sizes, shapes, and colors. If you're not Jewish, you're a Gentile, too!

Feature

KING DAVID BUILDS AN EMPIRE

When David became king, Saul had just lost a big battle, and Israel was overrun by Philistines. Within 20 years, David controlled a huge empire that stretched from Egypt to the Euphrates River. How did he do it? Well, God did miracles to help him, the Israelites learned how to make iron weapons, *and* David was a superwarrior! It was one battle after another—each victory bigger and more spectacular than the last—until finally David was the undisputed ruler over an empire. Five hundred years later, the Persians still remembered how powerful Israel had been. (See: 1 Samuel 31:7; 2 Samuel 8:1–14; Ezra 4:18–20.)

Three Biggest Gatherings of False Prophets

1. Ahab gathered 450 prophets of Baal.
2. Jehu killed a huge crowd of prophets and ministers of Baal.
3. Ahab gathered 400 false prophets.

(See: 1 Kings 18:19–20;
2 Kings 10:18–25;
2 Chronicles 18:5.)

I Love Lists!

Places & People

BETHLEHEM

The hometown of King David, son of Jesse. It was about five miles south of Jerusalem. Mary and Joseph traveled to Bethlehem to pay taxes, and Jesus was born there. (See: 1 Samuel 16:1; Luke 2:1–7.)

FUN FACTS!
Talk about the neighborhood going to the dogs. Jeremiah wrote that whenever Israelites abandoned their cities, guess who moved into the ruined houses? Jackals! (See: Jeremiah 9:11; 10:22.)

Bethlehem, where the "Prince of Peace" was born on the first Christmas, is a town now fought over by Jews and Palestinians.

FUN FACTS!
King Jeroboam was about to sacrifice to his idols when a prophet of God came along and prophesied against the altar. It immediately split in half. (See: 1 Kings 13:1–5.)

Who's that?

JESSE

The father of King David and ancestor of Jesus. Jesse was a well-to-do shepherd in Bethlehem who had eight sons and two daughters. David was his youngest son. (See: 1 Samuel 16:1–13; 17:12–19.)

JESUS

God's Son and the Son of Mary. Jesus went around Israel, preaching, teaching, and healing. He was crucified by His enemies but rose from the dead! (See: Matthew 1:18–25; 26–28; Acts 10:36–41.)

FUN FACTS!
A man named Sceva had seven sons who went around trying to cast out demons. They were pathetic and powerless, though, because they didn't really know Jesus. (See: Acts 19:13–16.)

STRANGE BUT TRUE!
The Midianite kings loved their camels, to be sure! Nothing was too good for the royal camels! They even hung gold chains around their camels' necks. (See: Judges 8:26.)

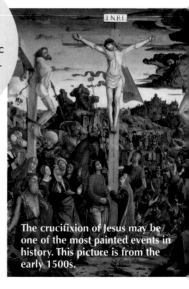

The crucifixion of Jesus may be one of the most painted events in history. This picture is from the early 1500s.

JETHRO

The priest of Midian, also called Reuel. His daughter, Zipporah, married Moses. Later on, Jethro gave Moses wise advice on how to get organized. (See: Exodus 2:15–21; 18.)

And that Definition Means...

GLORIFICATION

Glorification means "to share in Christ's glory" (Romans 8:17 NIV). Jesus had an incredible, glorious body after His resurrection. When believers are raised from the dead they will have new, eternal, glorious bodies, too. (See also Resurrection, page 90; see also: 1 Corinthians 15:40–44; Revelation 1:13–16.)

SADDUCEE

The Sadducees were leading men from wealthy families of priests. They believed in God but did not believe in angels or the resurrection from the dead. To the Sadducees, only this life was important. They were also really into the temple ceremonies. Jesus warned His disciples against the teachings of the Sadducees. (See: Matthew 16:5–12; Acts 23:8.)

Feature

HONOR GUARD OF HEAVENLY MONSTERS

When God, through Moses, commanded the Israelites not to make idols of any creature in heaven or in earth, He didn't mean that they couldn't make statues and carve images of the cherubim. These awesome, weird creatures were like an honor guard around God's throne. For a bizarre description of these many-winged, multi-eyed monsters, read Ezekiel 1:4–14 and Revelation 4:6–8. God's presence dwelled in the Holy of Holies (in the most inner part of the temple), so workmen placed two 15-foot-tall golden statues of cherubim there, and put two small cherubim on top of the Ark of the Covenant. They then carved cherubim all over the inside walls of the temple. (See: Exodus 20:4; 1 Kings 6:23–35.)

FUN FACTS!
King Manasseh was so foolish that he had priests burn incense to the sun, and made idols of a horse and chariot for the sun, too. He must have gotten a little too much sun. (See: 2 Kings 21:5, 23:11; 2 Chronicles 33:7.)

Places & People

NAZARETH

In Jesus' day, Nazareth was a small hilltop town in Galilee, north of Judea. Jesus grew up there as a child and, as a young man, was a carpenter there. (See: Matthew 2:22–23; Mark 6:3; Luke 1:26–27; 4:16.)

Seven Prophecies that Jesus Fulfilled

1. He was born in Bethlehem in Judea.
2. He was betrayed for 30 pieces of silver, which were then thrown down and used to buy a potter's field.
3. He was crucified ("pierced My hands and My feet") (Psalm 22:16 NKJV; Matthew 27:35 NKJV).
4. Enemies mocked Him, saying, "Let the LORD rescue him" (Psalm 22:7–8 NIV).
5. Men gambled for His clothes and divided them up.
6. He was buried in a rich man's grave.
7. He was dead for three days, then was raised to life.

(See: Psalm 22:18; Isaiah 53:9; Micah 5:2; Zechariah 11:12–13; Matthew 2:4–9; 20:18–19; 26:14–16; 27:3–10, 43, 57–60; 28:1–6; John 19:23–24.)

I love Lists!

An old-time carpentry shop in Italy.

JEZEBEL

The evil, Baal-worshipping wife of King Ahab of Israel. She tried to slay all God's prophets but was later killed by order of Jehu. (See: 1 Kings 19:1–2; 21; 2 Kings 9:30–37.)

JOAB

King David's nephew. For many years, Joab was the commander of David's army. He was a brave soldier but was also very rough and merciless. (See: 2 Samuel 3:22–30; 18:1–15; 20:4–10.)

JOASH

As a baby, Joash barely escaped being killed by his murderous grandmother, Athaliah. Joash was hidden in God's temple until, at age seven, he became the king of Judah. (See: 2 Chronicles 22:10–24:27.)

FUN FACTS!
Josiah was only eight years old when he became king of Judah. That wasn't even the record! Joash was only a seven-year-old kid when he became king. (See: 2 Kings 22:1; 2 Chronicles 24:1.)

DAY OF THE LORD

Also called the day of God or the day of God's wrath. In the Old Testament this was the long-awaited day when the Lord would rescue Israel from her enemies and punish evildoers. The New Testament teaches that Jesus will judge the wicked after He returns. (See: Second Coming, page 104; see also: Isaiah 2:12–21; 2 Peter 3:10–13; Revelation 6:12–17.)

THE QUEEN OF SHEBA

The land of Sheba was down the Arabian coast from Israel, and in King Solomon's day it was ruled by a queen. We don't know her name, but we do know what she was very, very curious. When Solomon's ships passed her country, sailing to Ophir, she heard how wise he was, so she put together a huge caravan, loaded the camels down with spices and four and a half tons of gold, and rode 1,300 miles north to Israel. Once she got there, she peppered Solomon with hard questions and he answered them all. A thousand years later, Jesus praised the Queen of Sheba. (See: 1 Kings 9:26–28; 10:1–13; Matthew 12:42.)

FUN FACTS!
How rich was King Solomon? Every year his income was 666 "talents" of gold. That's 25 tons of gold! (See: 1 Kings 10:14.)

People in Bible times didn't like dogs. Would you like dogs if they all looked like this?

Six Verses about Dirty Dogs of Canaan

1. Dogs lapped up the blood of King Ahab, after he died.
2. Dogs ate most of Queen Jezebel, after she fell out a window.
3. Dogs prowled around cities, snarling and looking for food.
4. Some dogs are so lazy they can't be bothered to bark.
5. Dogs licked the oozing sores of a beggar.
6. Dogs vomit on the ground, then slurp it back up.

(See: 1 Kings 22:35–38; 2 Kings 9:34–36; Psalm 59:6; Isaiah 56:10–11; Luke 16:21; 2 Peter 2:22.)

I Love Lists!

Places & People

HEBRON

Hebron is a mountain city in the south of Israel. Abraham and Isaac lived there, and David ruled as king there for seven and a half years. (See: Genesis 13:18; 35:27; 2 Samuel 2:11.)

FUN FACTS!
David once sent some officials to Ammon, but the Ammonites shaved off half of every man's beard. David's men were so embarrassed that they didn't return to Jerusalem till their beards grew out. (See: 2 Samuel 10:1–5.)

Bars of gold sit on shelves in a heavily-guarded bank vault.

JOB

A very wealthy, righteous man who lived in the land of Uz. God allowed Satan to take away all of Job's riches—and even his health—to test Job's love for God. (See: Job 1:1–2:10.)

Job gets bad news—he's lost all of his animals, and even worse, his children!

JOEL

A prophet who wrote the book of Joel. We know nothing about Joel, his life, or even when he lived. Joel is famous for writing about an astonishing locust plague. (See: Joel 1:1–12; 2:1–11.)

JOHN

One of Jesus' 12 apostles and the brother of James. John outran Peter to Jesus' tomb and later wrote the Gospel of John, the book of Revelation, and three other biblical letters. (See: Mark 1:19–20; John 20:1–9.)

STRANGE BUT TRUE!
Have you ever seen a beast with two curling ram's horns, coming up out of the ground? John did! And it gets stranger still! This monster sounded like a dragon! (See: Revelation 13:11.)

DEMONS

Also called evil spirits or devils, demons follow the devil and seek to do evil to humans. In the beginning, demons were angels who joined Satan in a rebellion against God and fell with him. Demons don't have physical bodies but are spiritual forces of evil who live in the spiritual realms. (See: Matthew 8:16; Ephesians 6:12; Revelation 12:7–10.)

JUDAH AND ISRAEL—THE NATION DIVIDES

When King Solomon was old, he foolishly worshipped other gods, and this angered God. One day Jeroboam, one of Solomon's officials, was walking down the road out of Jerusalem when who should meet him but the prophet Ahijah wearing a new wool cloak! While Jeroboam watched in surprise, Ahijah ripped his cloak into 12 strips—he was strong—then told Jeroboam to take ten pieces. He explained that God would make Jeroboam king over the ten northern tribes of Israel and only leave Judah and parts of some other tribes for Solomon's descendants to rule over. Sure enough, that's what happened. (See: 1 Kings 11:26–37; 12:1–17.)

Places & People

JERUSALEM

Jerusalem was once named Jebus, but King David made it the capital of Israel and called it Jerusalem, the City of David. Later on, King Solomon built God's temple there. (See: 2 Samuel 5:6–9; 1 Kings 6:1.)

Five Cases of the Most Animals Sacrificed at Once— Listed from Most to Least

1. King Solomon: so many sheep and cattle that they couldn't be counted
2. King Solomon: 22,000 cattle and 120,000 sheep and goats
3. King Josiah and his officials: 37,600 sheep and goats and 3,800 cattle
4. King Hezekiah: 600 bulls and 3,000 sheep and goats
5. Governor Tattenai: 100 bulls, 200 rams, 400 lambs, 12 goats

(See: 1 Kings 8:5, 63; 2 Chronicles 29:31–33; 35:7–9; Ezra 6:13, 17.)

STRANGE BUT TRUE!
The Bible talks about an astonishing, fire-breathing swamp monster called *leviathan*. Read all about it in Job 41. Was it real or symbolic? No one knows for sure.

THE NAME GAME!
In the Bible, a man's sons were almost always named, but his daughters usually weren't. But Job's three daughters *were* named and his seven sons *weren't*. (See: Job 42:13–14.)

FUN FACTS!
Where do locusts hide out on a cold day? The King James Bible says they hide inside hedges. The New International Version says they crawl into holes in walls. They actually do both. (See: Nahum 3:17.)

JOHN THE BAPTIST

The prophet who prepared the way for Jesus. John had an amazing birth, baptized Jesus, and was later imprisoned and beheaded. (See: Luke 1:5–25, 80; John 1:19–34; Mark 6:17–29.)

JONAH

A prophet of northern Israel. God told him to warn Nineveh, but Jonah ran away instead, got caught in a storm, and ended up in the belly of a great fish for three days. (See: Jonah 1.)

JONATHAN

The son of King Saul. Prince Jonathan was a brave, godly warrior and David's closest friend. He stepped aside so that David could be king instead of him. (See: 1 Samuel 14; 18:1–4; 23:16–18.)

BAPTISM, BAPTIZE

John the Baptist baptized sinners who repented. Jesus' disciples also told people, "Repent, and be baptized" (Acts 2:38 KJV). New Christians were baptized soon after they accepted Jesus. Being baptized doesn't save us, but it's an important way of showing publicly that we have had an inward change. (See: Matthew 3:5–6; Acts 2:41; 1 Peter 3:21.)

SHISHAK'S SHATTERING INVASION

Egypt had a peace treaty with Israel—after all, David's son, King Solomon, had married Pharaoh's daughter—but then there was a dynasty change and a new pharaoh, Shishak, came to the throne. Shishak thought a *lot* about the 25 tons of gold that Solomon collected every year, so after Solomon died and Rehoboam was king, Shishak launched a surprise attack. The Israelites were disobeying God big time so He didn't protect them, and next thing you know, the Egyptian army was parked outside Jerusalem. Rehoboam repented, so God spared him, but he *did* have to hand over all the gold to Shishak. (See: 1 Kings 3:1; 10:14–16; 14:21–26; 2 Chronicles 12:1–13.)

FUN FACTS!
Hundreds of years after the Israelites left Egypt, the Egyptians invaded Israel, ruled it, and made Israel pay them huge amounts of gold. They did this *twice!* (See: 2 Chronicles 12:1–9; 36:1–4.)

Places & People

ASSYRIA (ASSYRIANS)

Assyria was a giant empire that conquered most of the Middle East, including Israel. Their capital, Nineveh, was a huge city. The Assyrians were very cruel. (See: 2 Kings 17:1–6; Jonah 1:2; 4:11.)

A bird-like god of the Assyrians.

Seven Hebrews Who Married Egyptians

God commanded His people not to marry Canaanites but *didn't* say not to marry Egyptians:

1. Abraham took Hagar the Egyptian as a wife.
2. Hagar found an Egyptian wife for her son, Ishmael.
3. Joseph married Asenath, the daughter of an Egyptian priest.
4. An Israelite woman married an Egyptian.
5. Solomon married Pharaoh's daughter.
6. Sheshan let his daughter marry their Egyptian servant, Jarha.
7. Mered married Bithia, Pharaoh's daughter.

(See: Genesis 16:1–4; 21:21; 41:45; Leviticus 24:10; 1 Kings 3:1; 1 Chronicles 2:34–35; 4:18.)

I Love Lists!

FUN FACTS!
Jacob and his sons were shepherds, but when they moved to Egypt that was a bit of a problem, since the Egyptians *hated* shepherds. (See: Genesis 46:31–34.)

FUN FACTS!
The Israelites really enjoyed the melons of Egypt. When they arrived in Canaan they grew watermelons, cantaloupes, and honeydew melons. (See: Numbers 11:5.)

JORAM

The son of King Ahab and Queen Jezebel, and an evil king of Israel. Joram was killed by a well-aimed arrow when he was fleeing in his chariot from Jehu. (See: 2 Kings 3:1–3; 9:14–24.)

JOSEPH OF ARIMATHEA

A wealthy disciple of Jesus and a friend of Nicodemus. After Jesus died, Joseph asked Pilate for His body, then buried Jesus in his own tomb. (See: Luke 23:50–53; John 19:38–42.)

JOSEPH

Jacob's favorite son. Joseph's jealous brothers sold him as a slave into Egypt, and Joseph suffered injustices there. Then God made Joseph the ruler of all Egypt. (See: Genesis 37, 39–41.)

FUN FACTS!
Joseph was the governor of Egypt. Everyone bowed down to him. Yet when he visited his father Jacob, he bowed down to *him*, his face down to the ground. (See: Genesis 41:40; 48:12.)

Joseph receives a report on food supplies in Egypt. God gave Joseph wisdom to prepare Egypt for a terrible famine.

RESURRECTION

To raise someone back to life after they have died and decayed—not in the same weak, mortal body, but in a changed, powerful new body that will live forever. Jesus was the first one to rise from the dead, and all Christians will be resurrected one day. This will happen at the Rapture, when Jesus comes back for us. (See: *Rapture*—below; see also: 1 Corinthians 15:20–21, 35–44, 51–52.)

RAPTURE

Also known as our "gathering together" (2 Thessalonians 2:1 KJV) to be with Christ. When Jesus returns in the clouds of heaven, Christians who have died will be resurrected first. Then we who are still alive will be "caught up together with them in the clouds" (1 Thessalonians 4:17 KJV). Angels will fly around the world, gathering us up. (See: *Resurrection*—above; see also: Matthew 24:31.)

Feature

HIDING IN KERITH CREEK
STRANGE BUT TRUE!

When King Ahab of Israel married Jezebel, an evil Canaanite, the prophet Elijah stomped into the palace, told Ahab that there would be no rain for three years, then left before the guards could stop him. God told Elijah to hide out in the valley of Kerith Creek, east of the Jordan River. Elijah drank from the brook until it ran dry, and ravens snatched food off people's tables and flew it to him twice a day. Meanwhile, Ahab was desperately searching for Elijah. He sent men to nations around Israel, making them swear that they couldn't find Elijah and weren't hiding him. They weren't. *God* was hiding him. (See: 1 Kings 17:1–6; 18:10–11.)

STRANGE BUT TRUE!
One time, in Elijah's day, a gully-washer of a heavy rainstorm began with a cloud as small as a man's hand, rising out of the sea. (See: 1 Kings 18:44–45.)

Four Raven Stories: the Good, the Bad, and the Ugly

1. Noah sent a raven out of the ark to see if the Flood had ended.
2. God commanded ravens to fly food to Elijah in a secret ravine.
3. Ravens peck out the eyes of disrespectful sons. Ouch!
4. God feeds the ravens, so we should trust God like they do.

(See: Genesis 8:6–7; 1 Kings 17:4–6; Proverbs 30:17; Luke 12

I Love Lists!

Places & People

A jet-black raven on desert rocks.

FUN FACTS!
Jacob arrived in Egypt and saw Joseph again when he was 130, but he never saw Joseph's two sons until 17 years later when he was dying. (See: Genesis 47:7–9, 28; 48:8–11.)

PHOENICIA (PHOENICIANS)

This land was on the sea coast north of Israel, and its most famous cities were Tyre and Sidon. Jezebel's father was a king of Phoenicia. Both Elijah and Jesus visited Phoenicia. (See: 1 Kings 16:31–17:24; Mark 7:24–30.)

FUN FACTS!
When Joseph was young, he was a strong-man, ruling Egypt with an iron hand. When he was old, he sat around cuddling newborn babies on his knees. (See: Genesis 50:22–23.)

Who's ? that?

JOSEPH

A carpenter of Nazareth and the husband of Mary. When King Herod wanted to kill baby Jesus, God warned Joseph in a dream to flee with Him to Egypt. (See: Matthew 1:18–2:23; 13:55.)

JOSHUA

The army commander under Moses. Joshua became leader of Israel after Moses died, and his great faith helped him to conquer Canaan. (See: Exodus 17:8–13; Deuteronomy 31:1–8; Joshua 11:18–23.)

JOSIAH

The last great, good king of Judah. When the Assyrian empire fell, Josiah reconquered northern Israel and rid the land of idols. He died in a battle against the Egyptians. (See: 2 Kings 22–23.)

Young Jesus holds a candle for his carpenter father, Joseph, in this painting from the 1600s.

FUN FACTS!
Amon was such an idol-worshipping king that when godly Josiah became king, it was a major cleanup job to get rid of all the idols Amon had set up. (See: 2 Kings 23:4–14.)

And that Definition Means...

GRACE

The kindness and favor of God toward man. Mary " 'found favor with God' " (Luke 1:30 NIV). *Grace* also means receiving God's favor and kindness when we don't deserve it. Paul talks a great deal about grace in the book of Galatians, and tells us that we are saved by God's grace—undeserved mercy—not by our own good works. (See: Ephesians 2:7–9.)

MERCY

Justice is when someone has offended you or has broken a law, and you punish them. *Mercy* is when you decided not to punish them. Jesus said, "Blessed are the merciful, for they shall obtain mercy" (Matthew 5:7 RSV). We were once spiritually dead, "but God, who is rich in mercy," (Ephesians 2:4 NKJV) has forgiven us and given us life. (See: Ephesians 2:4–5.)

Feature

GOAT-FLOCK ARMY ATTACKS

One time the king of Aram and his allies—32 kings and their armies—surrounded the city of Samaria. King Ahab had only 7,232 men, but a prophet of God told him to march out and attack, so he did, and defeated the monster army. (Even a bad king can do something right!) Next year the Arameans returned. They waited in the plains, basically saying, "Israel's gods are gods of the hills. That's why they defeated us last time." But God said that He would teach the Arameans that He was God of the plains, too. The Aramean army was so huge it covered the countryside, but the Israelites marched out "like two small flocks of goats" (1 Kings 20:27 NIV)—and defeated them again! (See: 1 Kings 20:1–30.)

STRANGE BUT TRUE!

Once Aramean and Israelite armies stared and glared at each other seven days before fighting. But the record goes to two armies who stood and stared at each other for 40 days. (See: 1 Kings 20:29; 1 Samuel 17:1–3, 16.)

AWESOME FEAT!

Once, the king of Aram got 32 other kings and their armies together and attacked Israel. But God helped Israel and all 33 kings lost! (See: 1 Kings 20:1, 19–21.)

FUN FACTS!

King Josiah hated idol worship so much that he dug up skeletons and burned the bones on pagan altars to make sure the altars were never used again. (See: 2 Kings 23:16.)

Ten Times People Built Altars to God

1. Noah built an altar after leaving the ark.
2. Abraham built an altar at Shechem.
3. Abraham built an altar near Bethel.
4. Abraham built an altar at Mamre near Hebron.
5. Abraham built an altar on Mount Moriah.
6. Isaac built an altar at Beersheba.
7. Joshua built an altar on Mount Ebal.
8. Samuel built an altar at Ramah.
9. David built an altar on Mount Moriah.
10. Elijah rebuilt an altar on Mount Carmel during King Ahab's day.

(See: Genesis 8:20; 12:6–8; 13:3–4, 18; 22:2, 9; 26:23–25; Joshua 8:30; 1 Samuel 7:15, 17; 2 Samuel 24:24–25; 1 Kings 18:20, 30–31; 2 Chronicles 3:1.)

I Love Lists!

Who's that?

JOTHAM

A good king of Judah. God made him powerful because he faithfully walked close to God. Jotham was a great builder. (See: 2 Kings 15:32–38; 2 Chronicles 27.)

JUDAH

One of the 12 sons of Jacob and the ancestor of the tribe of Judah. Judah gave Tamar his signet as a pledge. Their son, Perez, is an ancestor of both King David and Jesus. (See: Genesis 35:23; 38; Matthew 1:1–16.)

JUDAS ISCARIOT

One of Jesus' 12 apostles. Judas betrayed Jesus for 30 pieces of silver and led His enemies to Him. Judas later hanged himself. (See: Matthew 26:14–16, 47–50; 27:1–10; John 13:18–30.)

STRANGE BUT TRUE!
When Tamar was giving birth to twin boys fathered by Judah, one baby stuck his hand out, then for some reason backed up and let his brother be born first. (See: Genesis 38:27–30.)

Judas kisses Jesus, to show the armed crowd behind Him who to arrest.

And that Definition Means...

CROWN OF LIFE

Not a heavy crown like a king or queen's crown, but a laurel leaf "crown" that was given to the winner of ancient Greek Olympic competitions. Some people believe that the *crown of life* is eternal life given to those who remain faithful. Others believe that the crown is the reward that believers will receive for the good they have done. (See: James 1:12; Revelation 2:10.)

Feature

AHAB GOES DOWN WITH AN ARROW

Talk about tricky! Before heading into a battle, King Ahab asked a prophet of God for advice. The prophet said that because Ahab had done evil, he'd die in battle. Ahab threw the prophet in prison and rode his chariot out to battle. But he was worried that the prophet's words might come true so he took off his crown and royal robes and dressed like a common soldier. When they were in the battle—*whunk*!—a stray arrow hit him right between the spaces of his armor. Ahab was wounded but thought he'd survive, so he watched the battle all day. . .but by evening he was dead. (See: 1 Kings 22:1–40.)

Places & People

JEWS

Jew originally meant Israelites of the tribe of Judah. After the Babylonians carried them away to Babylon, *Jew* came to mean *any* Israelite, whether they were from Judah or not. For example, Mordecai was "a Jew of the tribe of Benjamin" (Esther 2:5 NIV).

FUN FACTS!
Men once "signed" documents using signets—cylinder seals with drawings carved on them. When they rolled it across a moist clay tablet it printed the drawing there. (See: Genesis 38:18.)

FUN FACTS!
When Joseph was ruling Egypt, and his father Jacob still lived in Canaan, Joseph sent his dad ten donkeys loaded down with the best Egyptian presents. (See: Genesis 45:23.)

A donkey awaits a tourist rider in the middle eastern country of Jordan.

FUN FACTS!
When Pharaoh asked Jacob how old he was, Jacob replied that he was 130—then complained that he hadn't lived a very long life at all. (See: Genesis 47:7–9.)

Seven Unusual Things That Happened on Mountaintops

1. Abraham nearly sacrificed his son on Mount Moriah.
2. Moses met God on top of Mount Sinai.
3. Aaron, Moses' brother, died on Mount Hor.
4. Moses saw Canaan from Mount Nebo, then died there.
5. Joshua built an altar and read the Law on Mount Ebal.
6. Jotham shouted out a fable on top of Mount Gerizim.
7. Elijah called down fire on Mount Carmel during Ahab's reign.

(See: Genesis 22:1–14; Exodus 19:16–20; Numbers 20:23–28; Deuteronomy 34:1–5; Joshua 8:30–35; Judges 9:7–20; 1 Kings 18:20, 36–38.)

I Love Lists!

Who's that?

JUDE

Also known as *Judah* (Hebrew) and *Judas* (Greek). A brother of Jesus and James. At first, Jude didn't believe in Jesus. Later, he became a believer and wrote the book of Jude. (See: Matthew 13:55; John 7:5; Jude 1:1.)

KETURAH

Abraham's second concubine—or lesser wife. (Hagar was Abraham's first concubine.) Keturah bore Abraham six sons, the ancestors of Arabian tribes. (See: Genesis 25:1–6.)

KORAH

A Levite who led a rebellion against Moses in the Sinai wilderness. God judged Korah by having the earth open up to swallow him alive. (See: Numbers 16:1–34).

FUN FACTS!
Hebrews 1:10–12 says that though God lives forever, the heavens and the earth will grow old. They will wear out like old clothes, and God will roll them up like a worn-out robe.

THE NAME GAME!
One guy in Israel was named Becher (Genesis 46:21 KJV), which means "young camel." You can be sure Becher didn't name his son "Gemalli" (Numbers 13:12). *Gemalli* means "camel driver."

FUN FACTS!
The Israelites celebrated a feast at the beginning of every month when the moon was "new" (blacked out). They called it the New Moon Festival. (See: Numbers 10:10; 28:11; 1 Samuel 20:18).

THE NAME GAME!
In ancient Israel, if a girl owned a pony, chances are she'd name it *Susi*. Why? Because in Hebrew *Susi* means "my horse." There was once a *man* named "Susi" (Numbers 13:11).

And that Definition Means...

BELIEVE

To *believe* in God doesn't mean to simply agree that He exists. Even the devils do that. When the Old Testament says people *believe* in God, the Hebrew word used is *aman*, which means "to remain faithful." When the New Testament says to *believe* in Jesus, the Greek word used is *pisteuō*, which means "to stick to, trust, rely on." (See: Genesis 15:6; John 3:16; Acts 4:4; James 2:19).

INHERITANCE

In the Bible, an *inheritance* is property and belongings that sons (and sometimes daughters) received when their father died. God promised the land of Canaan to Abraham, so it was the inheritance of Abraham's children. Jesus promised that we would inherit eternal life in the Kingdom of God, and Peter said that we have an inheritance waiting in heaven for us. (See: Psalm 105:8–11; Matthew 25:34; 1 Peter 1:3–4.)

A crowd gathers in New York City to support Bobby Sands, an Irish soldier on a "hunger strike." In 1981, he went without food for 66 days before he died.

Three Men Who Went 40 Days without Eating Food

1. Moses
2. Elijah
3. Jesus

(See: Exodus 24:18; 34:28; 1 Kings 19:3–8; Matthew 4:1–2.)

Feature

102 SOLDIERS FRIED BY FALLING FIRE

When King Ahaziah of Israel was injured, he sent messengers to the Philistines to ask their god, Baal-Zebub, if he'd recover. Elijah sent this message to Ahaziah: "You will surely die!" Ahaziah sent a captain and 50 soldiers to arrest Elijah. They found him sitting on a hill. The captain ordered, "Man of God, the king has said, 'Come down!' " (2 Kings 1:9 NKJV). Instead, the soldiers were burned up by fire from heaven. The king sent a captain and 50 more soldiers. They were burned alive, too. Ahaziah sent another 50 soldiers. This time the captain begged for his men's lives, so Elijah went with him and told the king his message personally. (See: 2 Kings 1:1–17.)

MOUNT SINAI

Also called Mount Horeb, it rises in the deserts of the southern Sinai Peninsula. Moses saw the burning bush and received the Ten Commandments from God there. (See: Exodus 3:1–2; 31:18.)

Places & People

Who's that?

LABAN

Brother of Rebekah. Laban was tricky and greedy. He cheated his nephew Jacob by making him work seven years for Rachel, then giving him Leah instead. (See: Genesis 24:29–59; 29:13–30.)

LAZARUS

Brother of Mary and Martha. Lazarus became sick and died. After he'd been buried for four days, Jesus came to his village and raised him from the dead. (See: John 11:1–44; 12:1–2.)

LEAH

Daughter of Laban and sister of Rachel. Laban tricked Jacob by giving him Leah as his wife instead of Rachel. Leah bore Jacob six sons. (See: Genesis 29:15–35; 35:23.)

FUN FACTS!
"Are we there yet?" When the Israelites moved to Egypt, little kids like Hezron, Hamul, and Heber—Jacob's great-grandchildren—rode all the way there in carts. (See: Genesis 46:5, 12, 17.)

THE NAME GAME!
Jacob had a wife named *Leah*. Her name means "wild cow." Other women had names like that, too—David's wife *Eglah*, for example. Her name means "calf." (See: Genesis 29:32; 2 Samuel 3:5.)

THE NAME GAME!
Tola—now *there's* a guy's name you don't hear every day! Tola was Leah and Jacob's grandson, and his name means "worm" or "scarlet (the juice produced by worms)." Imagine your dad calling you Red Worm Juice. (See: Genesis 46:13.)

And that Definition Means...

SIGNS AND WONDERS

Miracles that God does to draw attention to the gospel and the power of Jesus. The apostles performed "many signs and wonders" (Acts 5:12 NKJV) among the people. Philip performed many miraculous signs in Samaria. (See: Acts 8:5–7.)

Feature

A Tale of Two Robes

When Jesus died on the cross, the Roman soldiers gambled for His robe. There's a famous movie called *The Robe*, telling of the miracles that Jesus' robe did. The Bible doesn't actually talk about those, but hundreds of years earlier when Elijah needed to cross the Jordan River, he rolled up his cloak (robe), hit the water with it, and the river divided and they crossed on dry land. When Elijah was caught up to heaven, Elisha inherited his cloak. Elisha walked up to the Jordan River and struck the water with his robe, and lo and behold, the water parted again and Elisha crossed back over. (See: John 19:23–24; 2 Kings 2:1–14.)

Places & People

Red Sea

The Red Sea lies to the east of Egypt, and one branch of it separates Egypt from the Sinai Peninsula. Through Moses, God parted the Red Sea to let the Israelites cross through it. (See: Exodus 14.)

Six Gravity-Defying Miracles

1. Moses divided the Red Sea and it became two walls of water.
2. Elijah and Elisha caused the Jordan River to part "to the one side and to the other" (2 Kings 2:8 RSV).
3. Elisha made an iron ax-head float on top of the water.
4. Jesus walked on top of the storm-tossed waves.
5. Peter also walked on the waves—for a little while.
6. Jesus ascended (rose up) into the sky.

(See: Exodus 14:21–22, 29; 2 Kings 6:5–7; Matthew 14:25–26, 28–29; Luke 24:50–51.)

I Love Lists!

Sunset over the Red Sea.

Who's that?

LEVI

One of the 12 sons of Jacob and ancestor of the Levites (priests whose rules are covered in the book of Leviticus) of the tribe of Levi. Levi and his brother Simeon attacked and killed every man in Shechem. (See: Genesis 34.)

STRANGE BUT TRUE!
Weasels, rats, geckos, and chameleons were considered unclean. If one of them dropped dead on an Israelite's oven, she had to break her oven in pieces. (See: Leviticus 11:29–30, 35.)

REALLY GROSS!
God warned the Israelites twice that if they didn't obey Him, the very land of Israel would "vomit" (Leviticus 18:28; 20:22 NKJV) them out.

LOT

Abraham's nephew Lot traveled with Abraham to Canaan. When they separated, Lot moved to Sodom. Abraham rescued him once; angels rescued him again. (See: Genesis 12:4–5; 13–14; 19.)

LUKE

A Greek doctor. Luke was a faithful friend of Paul, who often traveled with him. Luke wrote the Gospel of Luke and the book of Acts. (See: Colossians 4:14; 2 Timothy 4:9–11.)

FUN FACTS!
The apostle Paul wrote that he had been shipwrecked three times. After he wrote that, he was shipwrecked for the *fourth* time! (See: Acts 27:41–44; 2 Corinthians 11:25.)

And that Definition Means...

TITHING

Tithing means giving God one-tenth of your earnings. In the Old Testament, the Law required the Jews to bring their tithes to the Levites in the temple. God promised to bless them if they tithed. Some people believe that Christians today must tithe. Others believe that the "one-tenth" law no longer applies, but that Christians should give generously. (See: Malachi 3:8–10; 2 Corinthians 9:6–8.)

Feature

ELISHA AND THE POISONOUS STEW

When Elisha was staying at Gilgal (near Jericho) some prophets gathered to learn from him. Elisha told his servant, "Put on the large pot and cook some stew." One clueless guy wandered through a nearby field, gathering herbs for flavoring, and stumbled upon some gourds. They *looked* good, so he cut them up and stirred them into the stew. When the prophets began to eat, they realized that the stew was poisoned! Elisha threw some flour in the pot and said, "Pour out for the men, that they may eat" (2 Kings 4:41 RSV). It took huge faith for them to try again, but God did a miracle and they were fine. (See: 2 Kings 4:38–41.)

Three Times People Moved to New Lands because of Their Animals

1. Abraham and Lot separated because they had too much livestock.
2. Jacob and Esau had so many flocks and herds they had to live in separate lands.
3. The sons of Simeon had to move to Gedor to find pasture for their flocks.

(See: Genesis 13:5–12; 36:6–7; 1 Chronicles 4:34–40.)

I Love Lists!

You wouldn't want to put these pretty, but poisonous, toadstools in your soup!

LYDIA

A Jewish woman who lived in Philippi, Greece. Lydia imported purple cloth from Thyatira and resold it. She became a Christian and took Paul and Silas into her home, where they fellowshipped. (See: Acts 16:12–15; 40.)

MALACHI

A prophet who wrote the book of Malachi, the last book in the Old Testament. He lived in the days of Nehemiah, after the Jews had returned from Babylon to Judah. (See: Malachi 1:1.)

FUN FACTS!
When the Israelites offered blind and lame animals to God, God replied through Malachi, "Try offering them to your governor! Would he be pleased with you?" (Malachi 1:8 NIV).

MARK

Also called John Mark. Mark joined his cousin Barnabas and Paul on their first missionary trip, then deserted them. Later he worked with Paul again. He wrote the Gospel of Mark. (See: Acts 12:25; 13:13; Colossians 4:10; 2 Timothy 4:11.)

FELLOWSHIP

Fellowship means "partnership." Christians have fellowship with Jesus. When believers work together to do God's will, encourage one another, or gather to worship God and study His Word, this is also called fellowship. The Bible tells us that it's important for Christians to fellowship regularly with each other. (See: Acts 2:42; 1 Corinthians 1:9; Hebrews 10:25.)

REDUCING A TEMPLE TO RUBBLE

When Jehu became the new king of Israel, he had a huge problem. He had wiped out the old Baal-worshipping king and queen, but there were still hundreds of prophets and ministers and priests of Baal in Israel, teaching people to worship Baal. Jehu was quite crafty, however, and he called them all together to a special festival for Baal. When they filled the temple of Baal, he had them all killed. He then took out the "sacred pillar of Baal" (2 Kings 10:27 NKJV) and smashed it to bits. After that, he had the temple of Baal torn down. For hundreds of years afterwards, people used the ruins as a public toilet. (See: 2 Kings 10:18–28.)

FUN FACTS!
Job made it clear that he was not one of those weird sun-worshippers who blew kisses to the sun and the moon. (See: Job 31:26–28.)

What drought does to the landscape. This scene is from Africa.

Seven Deadly, Dry Droughts and Fierce Famines

1. The drought and severe famine in Abraham and Lot's day
2. The drought and famine in Isaac's day
3. The drought and famine in Joseph's day
4. The drought and famine in Ruth's day
5. The three-year famine in King David's day
6. The drought and famine in Nehemiah's day
7. The severe drought and famine in Claudius's day

(See: Genesis 12:10; 26:1; 41:53–55;Ruth 1:1; 2 Samuel 21:1; Nehemiah 5:3; Acts 11:28.)

Places & People

MOAB (MOABITES)

Moab was a son of Lot, and Moab's descendants, the Moabites, lived in the land of Moab east of the Dead Sea. Eglon, king of Moab, invaded Israel. (See: Genesis 19:36–37; Judges 3:12–30.)

STRANGE BUT TRUE!

When Ehud killed the dictator Eglon, Eglon's servants waited and waited *and waited* before entering the room. They thought Eglon was on the toilet the whole time. (See: Judges 3:20–25.)

REALLY GROSS!

During one famine, people were so hungry they ate dove's poop. At least that's what the King James Bible indicates, using the word "dung" (2 Kings 6:25). The New International Version says they ate "seed pods."

MARTHA

The sister of Mary and Lazarus, of the village of Bethany. Martha worked hard—sometimes too hard—but she loved Jesus and had great faith in Him. (See: Luke 10:38–42; John 11.)

Martha (left), busy with work, looks angrily at her sister, Mary, spending quiet time with Jesus.

MARY MAGDALENE

A devoted believer who gave money to support Jesus. She bravely stood at His cross when He died and was the first one to see Him after His resurrection. (See: Luke 8:1–3; John 19:25; 20:1–18.)

MARY

The mother of Jesus and the wife of Joseph. The angel Gabriel told Mary that she would give birth to the Son of God, and she believed him. (See: Luke 1:26–38; 2:1–7, 21.)

SECOND COMING

After Jesus was crucified, He was resurrected and went to heaven to be with His Father. One day, He will return in the clouds of heaven and rapture all believers. He will then judge the world and set up His kingdom on earth. Jesus came the first time as a baby, but when He appears the second time, He will come to save and resurrect us! (See: Matthew 24:29–31; Hebrews 9:28.)

WITNESS

A witness is someone who testifies (speaks publicly) about the things he knows to be true. Peter refused to stop talking about Jesus and His resurrection, saying, "We cannot help speaking about what we have seen and heard" (Acts 4:20 NIV). Christians today are also commanded to witness to others that the gospel is true. (See Preach, page 124; see also: Mark 16:15.)

Feature

THE PRINCESS AND THE WITCH QUEEN

After King Ahaziah of Judah died, one of his sons should've become king, but Ahaziah's evil mother, Athaliah, decided that *she* wanted to be queen. To be sure that no one would challenge her, she sent soldiers from room to room throughout the palace, killing all her grandsons! Ahaziah's sister, however, got wind of the plot and—just in time—grabbed baby prince Joash and his nanny and hid them in another room. Then when it was safe, she smuggled them out of the palace and into God's temple. Joash was hidden there for six years until it was time for him to be declared the rightful king. (See: 2 Kings 11.)

FUN FACTS!
Digging a well was hard work and was usually done by servants. When some nobles and princes dug a well, a song was made up to remember the rare event. (See: Numbers 21:17–18.)

Places & People

BETHANY

Bethany was a Jewish village less than two miles east of Jerusalem, on the other side of the Mount of Olives. Jesus' friends Lazarus, Mary, and Martha lived there. (See: John 11:1–2, 18.)

FUN FACTS!
One time Elah, king of Israel, was getting drunk in a friend's house when Zimri, one of his army officers, walked in and killed him. Then Zimri became king. (See: 1 Kings 16:8–10.)

THE NAME GAME!
There's a famous book and movie called *Ben-Hur* about a man who lived in Jesus' day. The real Ben-Hur lived in King Solomon's day, 900 years earlier. (See: 1 Kings 4:8.)

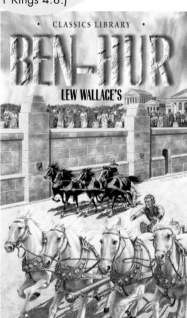

CLASSICS LIBRARY
BEN-HUR
LEW WALLACE'S

Three Kings Who Were Killed in Their Beds

1. King Ish-Bosheth
2. King Ben-Hadad
3. King Joash

(See: 2 Samuel 4:5–7; 2 Kings 8:14–15; 2 Chronicles 24:25.)

I Love Lists!

Who's that?

MARY

The sister of Martha and Lazarus of Bethany. Mary sat at Jesus' feet, listening to Him teach, and later poured expensive perfume on His feet. (See: Luke 10:38–42; John 12:1–7.)

MATTHEW

One of Jesus' twelve apostles. Matthew was a tax collector and was also known as Levi. He wrote the Gospel of Matthew. (See: Matthew 9:9–13; Mark 2:13–17.)

MELCHIZEDEK

The king of Jerusalem in Abraham's day. Melchizedek was also a priest of God. The book of Hebrews says that Jesus is a high priest like Melchizedek. (See: Genesis 14:17–20; Hebrews 7:1–17.)

FUN FACTS!
Biggest tithe in the Bible: Abraham once gave Melchizedek, the king (and priest) of Jerusalem, one-tenth of the riches of two wealthy cities. (See: Genesis 14:11–16, 20.)

And that Definition Means...

PHARISEE

Pharisees means "the separate ones." The Pharisees were a group of Jews who tried very had to be righteous by following all of God's commandments and keeping separate from sinners. Some Pharisees were self-righteous hypocrites. Many Pharisees, however, were good people. They believed in God, in angels, and in the resurrection from the dead (Matthew 23; Acts 23:6–9).

HYPOCRITE

The Greek word *hypokritēs* meant "someone who acts a part in a play." Jesus used this word to describe religious people who were just acting, pretending to be godly when they really weren't. Paul described it as "having a form of godliness but denying its power" (2 Timothy 3:5 NIV) and talked about people who say they know God, but live ungodly lives. (See: Matthew 23:13–15; Titus 1:16.)

These masks symbolize the theater.

Eight Times All the Treasure in the Temple Was Taken

1. Pharaoh Shishak stripped the temple in King Rehoboam's day.
2. King Joash gave Hazael, king of Aram, all the temple gold.
3. King Jehoash took all the gold in King Amaziah's day.
4. King Ahaz sent the Assyrian king all the temple's silver and gold.
5. Sennacherib, king of Assyria, took all the temple's silver and gold in King Hezekiah's day.
6. Nebuchadnezzar, king of Babylon, took the temple treasure in Jehoiachin's day.
7. The Babylonians melted and took the gold, along with silver and bronze items from the temple, in Zedekiah's day.
8. King Asa gave Aramean king Ben-Hadad all the silver and gold in the temple's treasury.

(See: 1 Kings 14:25–26; 2 Kings 12:17–18; 14:11–14; 16:7–8; 18:14–16; 24:12–13; 25:13–17; 2 Chronicles 16:2–4.)

I Love Lists!

Feature

Two "Arrow Prophecies"

When Elisha was old, he became sick. One day Jehoash, king of Israel, visited him. Elisha told Jehoash to grab a bow and some arrows, then Elisha put his hands over the king's hands, and together they shot an arrow out the window. "The arrow of the Lord's victory over Aram!" Elisha shouted. Then Elisha told the king to smack the other arrows on the ground. Jehoash struck three times and stopped, but Elisha said, "You should have struck the ground five or six times; then you would have defeated Aram and completely destroyed it. But now you will defeat it only three times" (2 Kings 13:19 NIV). And that's what happened. (See: 2 Kings 13:14–19, 25.)

FUN FACTS!
The Pharisees in Jesus' day gave God one-tenth of their tiny garden spices—mint, dill, and cummin—but missed out on more important stuff, like loving their fellow man. (See: Matthew 23:23.)

MEPHIBOSHETH

The son of Prince Jonathan, David's best friend. Years after Jonathan had died, David showed great kindness to Mephibosheth. (See: 1 Samuel 20:42; 2 Samuel 9.)

MESHACH

Nebuchadnezzar threw Shadrach, Meshach, and Abednego into a fiery furnace for refusing to worship his idol, but God protected them. The king then made them officials of Babylon. (See: Daniel 3.)

MICAH

The prophet who wrote the book of Micah. He prophesied against Jerusalem in King Hezekiah's day, but the king repented, so God put off the judgment. (See: Micah 1:1; Jeremiah 26:18–19.)

FUN FACTS!
Once the people of Jerusalem were so rotten that God said, "I will wipe Jerusalem as one wipes a dish, wiping it and turning it upside down" (2 Kings 21:13 NKJV).

If you were asked to choose a real fruit—apples, oranges, cherries, and so on—for each of the nine fruits of the spirit, which would you choose? Why?

FRUIT OF THE SPIRIT

The *fruits of the Spirit* are the virtues (good qualities) that we should have when God's Holy Spirit lives in our lives. These virtues are love, joy, peace, patience, kindness, goodness, faithfulness, gentleness, and self-control. (See: Galatians 5:22–23.)

BLASPHEME, BLASPHEMY

To *blaspheme* does not simply mean to say a swear word. To *blaspheme* is to "take God's name in vain," to either say His name disrespectfully, mock God, or to say things about Him that aren't true. The high priests accused Jesus of blasphemy when He said that He was God's Son. Jesus wasn't blaspheming, however. He really *was* God's Son. (See: Exodus 20:7; Matthew 26:63–65.)

Feature

HEZEKIAH AND AN ANGEL AGAINST ASSYRIA

King Hezekiah of Judah paid the Assyrians 11 tons of silver and a ton of gold to leave him alone. That satisfied them for a while, but soon they were back. Their armies surrounded Jerusalem and they shouted to the soldiers of Jerusalem, "Do not let Hezekiah persuade you to trust in the LORD" (2 Kings 18:30 NIV)! The Assyrians boasted about all the other "gods" they had defeated and boasted that they would defeat Israel's God, too. Hezekiah prayed and reminded God that the Assyrians had ridiculed and blasphemed Him. God answered. That night He sent an angel into the Assyrian army camp and slaughtered 185,000 soldiers. (See: 2 Kings 18:13–19:37.)

Six Battles Where the Most People Died at Once—Listed from Most to Least

1. The army of Judah killed 500,000 men of Israel.
2. An angel of God killed 185,000 Assyrian soldiers.
3. The army of Israel killed 120,000 men from Judah.
4. David and the Israelites killed 40,700 Aramean invaders.
5. David and the Israelites killed 22,000 Arameans of Damascus.
6. The Israelites killed 25,100 Benjamite warriors.

(See: Judges 20:35; 2 Samuel 8:5; 10:18; 2 Kings 19:35; 2 Chronicles 13:17; 28:6.)

Four Leopard Spottings in Israel

Leopards once lived in Israel and were even more dangerous than lions.

1. Leopards often lived in the mountains.
2. Once, leopards waited near cities to maul anyone who came out the gates.
3. Leopards can't change their spots. Not that they *want* to.
4. Leopards sometimes lurked in ambush by the sides of roads.

(See: Song of Solomon 4:8; Jeremiah 5:6; 13:23; Hosea 13:7.)

STRANGE BUT TRUE!
When the Israelites were carried away captive, the king of Assyria moved foreigners into their land. But because they didn't worship God, He sent lions to kill some of them. (See: 2 Kings 17:24–25.)

MICAIAH

A true prophet of God who lived in Samaria. When King Ahab asked Micaiah about his plans to go to battle, Micaiah predicted disaster—and it happened. (See: 1 Kings 22:1–38.)

MICHAEL

An archangel ("the great prince") whose job is to watch over the Jewish people. Michael overcame a demon that was influencing Persia and also had an argument with Satan over the body of Moses. (See: Daniel 10:13; 12:1; Jude 1:9.)

MICHAL

Daughter of Saul and first wife of David. They were separated for many years. Michal had no children because she mocked David. (See: 1 Samuel 18:20–27; 25:44; 2 Samuel 3:12–16; 6:16–23.)

FUN FACTS!
Once King Saul sent men to arrest David, but David's wife Michal said that he was sick in bed. Saul answered, "Bring him up to me in the bed, that I may kill him" (1 Samuel 19:15 NKJV).

Michael the archangel kills a demon with a sword in this illustration from a book of the 1400s.

EDIFY, EDIFICATION

A term used often in the King James version of the Bible. To *edify* means to "build up" or to strengthen. Believers were often told to "build each other up" (1 Thessalonians 5:11 NIV) spiritually by speaking wise and loving things. Paul said that just having knowledge simply "puffs up," while having love actually "builds up" (1 Corinthians 8:1 NIV).

FUN FACTS!
The people of Samaria used to sift the chaff from the grain on a threshing floor right in front of the city gate, and sometimes Kings Ahab and Jehoshaphat would sit on their thrones there. (See: 1 Kings 22:10.)

Feature

BROKEN-DOWN CITY UNDER SIEGE

Nehemiah asked the king of Persia to let him go back to Jerusalem to rebuild its broken-down walls and its gates, which had burned down, and the king agreed. However, enemies like Sanballat did everything in their power to stop the Jews' work—so Nehemiah had guards watch the city day and night. Sanballat didn't give up. He threatened to mount a sudden attack and kill all the workers. After that, Nehemiah's builders carried tools in one hand and weapons in the other. They worked from dawn till sunset and slept in their clothes so they'd be ready to fight all the time. Finally they finished rebuilding the walls! (See: Nehemiah 2, 4.)

FUN FACTS!
In Nehemiah's day, some of the gates leading out of Jerusalem had odd names such as the Horse Gate, the Fish Gate, the Sheep Gate, and the Dung (or "Poop") Gate. (See: Nehemiah 3:14, 28; 12:39.).

Places & People

PERSIA (PERSIANS)

Persia, now called Iran, once had an empire that ruled much of the Middle East. A Jewish woman named Esther was the queen of the Persian king, Xerxes. (See: Esther 1:1; 2:5–7, 17.)

Colorful mosques—Muslim houses of worship—are among the well-known images of modern Iran.

Six Innocent People Who Were Lied About

1. Joseph's brothers lied that he had been killed.
2. Potiphar's wife lied that Joseph had tried to hurt her.
3. False witnesses lied that Naboth had cursed God and the king of Persia.
4. Sanballat lied that Nehemiah was rebelling against the king.
5. Jesus' enemies lied that He told the Jews not to pay taxes.
6. Paul's enemies made many serious false charges against him.

(See: Genesis 37:19–20, 31–33; 39:11–20; 1 Kings 21:7–13; Nehemiah 6:5–8; Luke 23:1–2; Acts 25:7.)

I Love Lists!

FUN FACTS!
When Nehemiah and the Jews returned to Jerusalem, most of the houses in the huge city were in ruins and empty. Must've been fun for kids to play hide-and-seek there. (See: Nehemiah 7:4.)

Who's ?
that?

MIRIAM

The older sister of Moses and Aaron, who looked out for baby Moses when his mother put him in a basket in Egypt's Nile River. Miriam was a prophetess but made the mistake of criticizing Moses. (See: Exodus 2:1–10; 15:20; Numbers 12.)

MORDECAI

Esther's cousin. Haman, King Xerxes's right-hand man, tried to kill Mordecai, but Haman was killed instead, and Mordecai took over his position. (See: Esther 2:5–7; 5:9–14; 7:9–8:2.)

MOSES

Moses, a Levite, was raised as a prince of Egypt but had to flee into the desert. He heard from God, came back as a miracle-working prophet, and freed the Israelite slaves. He then received the Law from God. (See: Exodus 2–3; 12:31–41; 32:15–16.)

AWESOME FEAT!
Moses sent 12,000 men to battle the Midianites, and they won. Not one Israelite died! The warriors were so impressed that they offered God 420 pounds of gold. (See: Numbers 31:5; 48–54.)

FUN FACTS!
The record for the most people becoming Jews at once goes to the Midianites. After one battle—in which no Israelites were killed—32,000 young Midianite women joined the nation of Israel. (See: Numbers 31:9, 32–35.)

Moses holds a stone tablet, containing the Ten Commandments, in this painting from the 1600s.

And that
Definition
Means...

SABBATH

God commanded the Jews to rest from their work one day a week, just as He himself had rested on the seventh day after creating the world. This day was called the Sabbath, which means "to cease working, to rest." Jews rest every Saturday. Most Christians rest on Sunday, however, because that's the day that God raised Jesus from the dead. (See Lord's Day, page 138; see also: Exodus 20:8–11.)

REALLY GROSS!
When God sent the plague of frogs on Egypt, they crawled and croaked all over the Egyptian people's houses, beds, ovens, and bread-making containers. (See: Exodus 8:2–4.)

Feature

FIXING A MESSED-UP ROYAL DECREE

Haman was the right-hand man of Xerxes, king of Persia, so when Haman told the king that there were some terrible, lawless people in his realm (he meant the Jews), Xerxes let Haman write a royal decree that all the Jews should be killed on a certain day. This law was sent to the entire empire. Then Queen Esther told the king that she herself was Jewish and asked King Xerxes to change his decree. The king wanted to, but no royal law could be changed. But he had an idea: Why didn't she write a *new* royal decree telling the Jews to defend themselves against their enemies? So she did, and they did! (See: Esther 3:8–15; 7:3–4; 8:1–17.)

Places & People

NILE RIVER

The longest river in Africa, it flows from Ethiopia (see Cush, page 45) north to Egypt. The civilization of ancient Egypt depended on its waters. God turned the Nile River into blood. (See: Exodus 7:14–20.)

21 of the Most Outstanding Lepers

1–2. Moses and Miriam were temporarily lepers.

3. God healed Naaman the Aramean from leprosy.

4. Gehazi received Naaman's leprosy for being greedy.

5–8. Four lepers outside Samaria announced great, good news.

9. King Azariah became a leper because of his pride.

10. Jesus had compassion on a leper and healed him.

11. Jesus stayed in the home of Simon the leper.

12–21. Jesus miraculously healed 10 lepers at once.

(See: Exodus 4:6–7; Numbers 12:9–15; 2 Kings 5:1–14, 20–27; 7:1–11; 15:1–5; 2 Chronicles 26; Matthew 8:1–3; 26:6; Luke 17:11–19.)

I Love Lists!

Who's that?

NAAMAN

The top commander of the army of Aram. The Arameans were Israel's enemies, but Naaman came to Israel to Elisha to be healed of leprosy. (See: 2 Kings 5:1–19; Luke 4:27.)

NABOTH

Naboth owned a vineyard near the palace of King Ahab. Ahab coveted Naboth's vineyard, so his wife Jezebel had Naboth falsely accused and killed so that Ahab could get it. (See: 1 Kings 21.)

FUN FACTS!
Once 200 warriors crouched and hid in the vineyards. When maidens came out to dance there at a festival, they jumped out and caught 200 of them for their wives. (See: Judges 20:47; 21:12–23.)

NAHUM

The prophet who wrote the book of Nahum. The Assyrians had destroyed northern Israel, but Nahum prophesied that God would destroy Nineveh, Assyria's capitol. (See: Nahum 1:1, 14; 2:1–10.)

FUN FACTS!
When the Israelites harvested their grapes, they couldn't check under the leaves twice for grapes they'd missed or pick up fallen grapes. They had to leave those for the poor. (See: Leviticus 19:10.)

A vineyard in Ontario, Canada.

And that Definition Means...

COVET, COVETOUS

To *covet* means to want something so bad that you can't stop thinking about it. To covet can be a good thing. Paul tells us to "covet" (1 Corinthians 12:31 KJV) or eagerly desire the gifts of God's Spirit. Usually, however, *covet* means to lust after something greedily. That's why Paul says that Christians shouldn't even have a tiny bit of covetousness. (See: Ephesians 5:3.)

YAHWEH

The personal name of God. Sometimes it's also pronounced "Jehovah" (Exodus 6:3 KJV; Psalm 83:18 KJV). To avoid accidentally speaking blasphemy against God, the Jews never pronounced this name, but whenever the name Yahweh appeared in the Bible, they read *Adonai* (Lord) instead. In most English Bibles, LORD (printed in what is called "capital and small capital letters") is written and used instead of God's actual name.

Feature

SATAN GETS TO PLAGUE JOB

Job was the wealthiest and godliest man in the land of Uz, but Satan insisted that Job only loved God because God had blessed him. Satan said that if Job lost everything he owned, Job would curse God—so God allowed Job to be tested. Next thing you know, Job's family was dead. His huge flocks and herds were gone. Job was devastated but he still praised God. Satan insisted that one final test would do it, so God allowed him to cover Job's body with painful, disgusting-looking sores. Job *still* refused to curse God. After Job had suffered awhile, God restored both his health and his wealth and blessed him more than ever before! (See: Job 1:1–2:10; 42:10–17.)

FUN FACTS!
Job said that he had often helped poor people and shared his food with them. He said that if this wasn't the truth he wanted his arm to fall off his shoulder. (See: Job 31:16–22.)

Six Amazing Women—with No Names!

1. Pharaoh's daughter who adopted Moses
2. Manoah's wife, the mother of Samson
3. The Queen of Sheba
4–5. Naaman's wife and (5) her Israelite slave girl
6. Isaiah's wife

(See: Exodus 2:1–10; Judges 13; 1 Kings 10:1; 2 Kings 5:2–3; Isaiah 8:3.)

I love Lists!

Places & People

MIDDLE EAST

All the lands from northern Africa in the west to Pakistan in the east. All the important Bible lands are here, including Egypt, Israel, Syria, and Persia (Iran).

STRANGE BUT TRUE!
In the book of Job, God talks about a monstrous beast named *behemoth* and says that "his tail sways like a cedar" (Job 40:17 NIV). What was *that*? Who knows? It sounds like an Ultrasaurus! (See: Job 40:15–24.)

A man stands underneath the skeleton of an Apatosaurus.

NAOMI

The mother-in-law of Ruth. During a famine, Naomi left Israel for Moab, where her husband and two sons died. Naomi returned to Israel with Ruth, and God blessed them both. (See: Ruth 1, 4.)

NATHAN

When King David asked if he should build a temple for God, the prophet Nathan said, "No." Nathan later rebuked David for killing Uriah and stealing his wife. (See: 2 Samuel 7:1–13; 12:1–25.)

THE NAME GAME!
"Hagab" (Ezra 2:46) and "Hagaba" (Nehemiah 7:48) were two men. Both of them were temple servants, and both their names meant "locust," a grasshopper-like bug.

NEBUCHADNEZZAR

The greatest king of Babylon. Nebuchadnezzar conquered Jerusalem and took the Jews as captives to Babylon. Daniel later interpreted his amazing dream. (See: 2 Kings 24–25; Daniel 1–4.)

King Nebuchadnezzar goes crazy, living like an animal for seven years, for his pride. See the whole story in Daniel 4.

LOVE

The two most important commandments are to love God with all our heart and soul and mind and to love our fellow man as ourselves. To *love* others means to treat them with the same kindness that we ourselves wish to be treated with. Paul said that we are fulfilling all the laws of God when we love others. (See: Matthew 7:12; 22:35–40; Galatians 5:14.)

IMPORTANT IDEA!
Too often people are prejudiced against foreigners, immigrants from foreign countries with different customs. But God told His people to *love* them. (See: Leviticus 19:34.)

FUN FACTS!
Israel was a fertile, rich land most of the time, and at times so many foreigners came there to find work and settled there that they grew into families and clans. (See: Leviticus 25:45.)

Feature

BARUCH AND THE BURNING SCROLL

A scribe named Baruch wrote down all the prophet Jeremiah's warnings in a scroll, then went to the temple and read them. Some of King Jehoiakim's officials heard him reading and told him that he and Jeremiah had better hide—so they did. Then the officials read the scroll to the king while he was sitting keeping warm in front of a fire pot. Every time they read a section, Jehoiakim, the servant king of Nebuchadnezzar of Babylon, cut it off with his knife and threw it in the fire. In the end, he had burned Jeremiah's entire scroll. God told Jeremiah not to worry. God gave him the warning prophecies again, and Baruch wrote them down again. (See: Jeremiah 36.)

Places & People

DEAD SEA

This large lake, also called the Salt Sea, is the lowest point on earth and is found on the western border of Moab. The Jordan River flows into the north end of it. The water is so salty that no fish can live there. (See: Genesis 14:3.)

Crusty salt collects on the shore of the Dead Sea.

Three Times Writings Were Destroyed or Lost

1. The long-lost Book of the Law was found.
2. King Jehoiakim burned the book of Jeremiah.
3. King Cyrus's decree about the Jews was found in Babylon.

(See: 2 Kings 22:8, 10; Jeremiah 36:21–23, 27–28; Ezra 5:17; 6:1–2.)

I Love Lists!

Three Unusual Bible Customs and Laws

1. The high priest sometimes dabbed ram's blood on his right ear lobe, on his big toe on the right foot, and on the thumb of his right hand.
2. If a man suspected his wife was sinning against him, she had to go to the temple and drink some holy water mixed with dust from the temple floor.
3. When buying someone's property, the sale wasn't legal until one person took off one of his sandals and gave it to the other person, which is how Boaz acquired Ruth and her land.

(See: Exodus 29:19–20; Numbers 5:11–31; Ruth 4:7.)

Who's that?

NEHEMIAH

A Jew and the official cupbearer (wine taster) for King Artaxerxes of Persia. The king made him the governor of Judah and sent him to rebuild the walls of Jerusalem. (See: Nehemiah 1:1–2:8; 5:14.)

FUN FACTS!
When he was governor of Judah, Nehemiah fed 150 guests and officials (not counting foreign visitors) a feast at his table *every day*—all at his own expense! (See: Nehemiah 5:17–18.)

NERO

Nero started out as a wise Caesar, which is why Paul chose to stand trial before him. Later Nero went insane and killed many Christians, including Peter and Paul. (See: Acts 25:9–11.)

This Roman coin, called a *denarius*, shows a picture of Nero.

FUN FACTS!
Where does the Bible talk about lots of children at the beach? In Acts 21:5—their families went to the harbor to say good-bye to Paul, and they all knelt on the beach and prayed.

NICODEMUS

A leading Pharisee who talked with Jesus about being born again. Nicodemus spoke up for Jesus and, after Jesus died, helped bury Him. (See: John 3:1–21; 7:47–52; 19:38–42.)

And that Definition Means...

BORN AGAIN

When Jesus talked with Nicodemus one night He told him, "You must be born again" (John 3:7 NIV). Jesus said that this was the same as being "born of the Spirit" (John 3:8 NIV). When we repent of our sins, put our faith in Jesus, and confess that Jesus is our Lord, the Spirit of Christ comes to live within our hearts. The Spirit gives us life and we are "born again" or "saved." (See: Romans 8:9–11; 10:9–10.)

Feature

GODLY GUY IN THE GOOEY MUD

When the Babylonians surrounded Jerusalem, Jeremiah told the Jews to make peace and surrender. This made some of King Zedekiah's advisers furious. King Zedekiah's son had a *cistern* (a huge water storage pit in the ground), but all the water was gone, and there was only mud in the bottom. The officials lowered Jeremiah into the mud and he would've died there except that a royal official, Ebed-Melech, got permission from the king to rescue him. Ebed lowered some old clothes down to Jeremiah, had him pad the ropes under his arms with them, then pulled the prophet back up out of the mud. (See: Jeremiah 38:1–13.)

Visitors to Israel today smear mud from the Dead Sea over their bodies—they think it's good for their health. Jeremiah's mud was a different thing entirely!

Six Times the Early Christians Were Beaten or Stoned

1. All 12 apostles were flogged (beaten with whips) in Jerusalem.
2. Stephen was stoned to death with rocks in Jerusalem.
3. Paul was stoned with rocks in Lystra and nearly died.
4. Paul and Silas were severely flogged in Philippi.
5. Paul was nearly beaten to death in Jerusalem.
6. Paul was beaten and suffered many times—see the full list in 2 Corinthians 11:23–26.

(See: Acts 5:27, 40; 7:57–60; 14:8–20; 16:12, 22–23; 21:30–32.)

I love Lists!

72 Men Who Were Chucked into Cisterns

Israel was a dry land, so the Israelites carved cisterns (huge water-storage pits) in the ground. They were not meant for storing *people*, but—

1. Joseph's jealous brothers threw him into a cistern.
2. The evil princes of Judah dropped Jeremiah into a cistern.
3–72. Seventy men from Israel were killed and thrown into a cistern.

(See: Genesis 37:23–24; Jeremiah 38:6; 41:4–8.)

Who's ? that?

NIMROD

A descendant of Noah's son Ham and the world's first empire-builder after the Flood. Nimrod was a "mighty warrior" (Genesis 10:8 NIV) and founded many cities. (See: Genesis 10:6–12.)

NOAH

Long ago, mankind was so wicked that God decided to flood the earth. He chose godly Noah to build an ark to save his family and animals of every species. (See: Genesis 5:28–32; 6–9.)

OBADIAH

A prophet who lived in Jeremiah's day and wrote a short prophecy against Edom. In fact, Obadiah 1:1–9 sounds *very* much like what Jeremiah wrote in Jeremiah 49:14–22.

FUN FACTS!
Noah's ark *was* actually huge enough to hold all those thousands of animals the Bible says it did. The ark was "450 feet long, 75 feet wide and 45 feet high" (Genesis 6:15 NIV).

What's wrong with this picture of Noah's ark? The Bible says it only had one window! (See Genesis 6:16.)

STRANGE BUT TRUE!
Some years after the Flood, a man named Arphaxad died 403 years after his first son, Shelah, was born—and Shelah died exactly 403 years after *his* first son was born! (See: Genesis 11:13, 15.)

FUN FACTS!
You know those bizarre fish that live in the bottom of the ocean, that have shiny eyes and are *all mouth*? God made them. He created every living thing in the seas. (See: Genesis 1:20–21.)

And that Definition → Means...

COVENANT

An agreement between two people or two nations, or between God and people. A covenant between nations is also called a treaty. A covenant between God and people is also called an agreement or a contract. God made a covenant with Noah. He also made a covenant with the nation of Israel. (See: Genesis 9:8–17; Exodus 24:3–8.)

SIN

Also known as *iniquity* or *transgression*. Anything that displeases God, anything that is unloving, anything that breaks God's laws. In the New Testament, *hamartia*, which is the Greek word for *sin*, means "to miss the mark." Since none of us are perfect, we have all missed the mark and sinned. (See: Romans 3:23.)

Feature

THE PERILOUS ADVENTURES OF THE ROYAL PRINCESSES

The Babylonians destroyed Jerusalem, burned the royal palace, then took King Zedekiah to Babylon and killed all his sons. Only his daughters were left, and they lived with the poor people in the town of Mizpah. Things were going fine until their cousin Ishmael came with ten men and kidnapped the princesses and everyone there. They were on their way to Ammon with them when Johanan and some Israelite soldiers caught up to Ishmael, drove him off, and then took the princesses and people and headed down to Egypt. Zedekiah's daughters were later part of the remnant of Judah that Johanan and the Israelite soldiers led into Egypt, where Jeremiah warned them of God's judgment. (See: Jeremiah 39:6–7; 40–41; 43:5–7.)

Places & People

MOUNTAINS OF ARARAT

Noah's ark landed on "the mountains of Ararat" (Genesis 8:4 KJV). These mountains are on the border of Turkey and Armenia.

Seven Facts about Israelite Cities

1. Each city had a well, often just outside the city.
2. City gates were closed and locked at night.
3. Cities had watchmen (lookouts) watching from the tops of walls.
4. Most cities sat on hilltops (mounds) for better defense.
5. Half-wild dogs hung around cities, eating garbage.
6. Cities had walls around them for protection.
7. Children played in the city streets.

(See: Genesis 24:13; Joshua 2:5; 1 Samuel 9:11; 2 Samuel 18:24; 1 Kings 16:24; 2 Kings 9:34–36; 2 Chronicles 14:7; Psalm 59:6; Zechariah 8:5.)

I Love Lists!

Mount Ararat rises above the city of Yerevan, Armenia.

Who's that?

Og

The giant king of Bashan (east of the Sea of Galilee). He's famous for having a monster-sized bed. The Israelites conquered Og's armies and took over his land. (See: Deuteronomy 3:1–11.)

Omri

A king of Israel, the northern kingdom. Omri fought a civil war against King Zimri, defeated him, and became king and the father of Ahab. Omri built a new capital city, Samaria, on a hill. (See: 1 Kings 16:15–28.)

Onesimus

A runaway slave who became a Christian. Paul wrote a letter to Philemon, Onesimus's master. He asked him to forgive Onesimus and to not treat him as a slave any longer. (See: Philemon 1.)

FUN FACTS!
Don't confuse Gog of Magog with Og of Argob. Gog is the chief prince of Magog—way up north.. Og was the giant king of Argob, near Israel. (See: Deuteronomy 3:4; Ezekiel 38:1–2.)

STRANGE BUT TRUE!
How big was the giant Og? When the Israelites entered his bedroom, they measured his bed and found it was 13½ feet long and 6 feet wide! Og was heavy, too! The bed was made of iron to support all his weight. (See: Deuteronomy 3:11.)

Statues of slaves in Stonetown, Zanzibar—a center of the slave trade in Africa. Little wonder that Onesimus ran away!

And that Definition Means...

Salvation, Saved

In the Old Testament, when the Jews prayed for God to save them or thanked Him for His salvation, they were usually talking about being saved from their enemies. In the New Testament, salvation means being saved from the fires of hell and being given eternal life. We are saved by believing in Jesus. (See: Psalm 44:6–7; Matthew 25:31–34, 41; Luke 1:71; John 3:16.)

Unity

Having *unity* means agreeing on the important things of the Christian faith and having enough love to agree to disagree on other minor issues. We can only have real unity when we treat each other with love and forgive each other. (See: 1 Corinthians 1:10; Romans 14:1–13; 1 Corinthians 12:25–26; Ephesians 4:32.)

Robbers are nothing new—they go way back to Bible times, too.

Four Cases of Missing Money

1. A man named Micah stole his mom's money and finally returned it.
2. Jesus talked about a dishonest manager who stole his master's wealth.
3. Judas kept the disciples' money bag and stole money from it.
4. Onesimus, a slave, stole money from his master.

(See: Judges 17:1–2; Luke 16:1; John 12:4–6; Philemon 1:18.)

Five Times Jesus Had Mercy on Despised Samaritans

1. Jesus talked with the Samaritan woman.
2. Jesus refused to take revenge on the Samaritans.
3. Jesus told the parable of the Good Samaritan.
4. Jesus healed and praised the Samaritan leper.
5. Jesus allowed Samaritans to receive salvation.

(See: John 4:7–9; Luke 9:51–56; 10:30–37; 17:11–19; Acts 1:8; 8:4–17.)

Feature

HANDWRITING ON THE PALACE WALL

In the days of King Belshazzar, God had had enough of the cruel Babylonian Empire. So one night when Belshazzar and all his court were having a big drunken feast—drinking wine out of the holy vessels of God's temple—a hand (just a hand!) appeared and wrote a message on the wall: MENE, MENE, TEKEL, PARSIN. Belshazzar was so scared that his face went pale and his knees knocked together. The prophet Daniel was brought in, and he interpreted the mysterious message. God was about to judge Babylon! Sure enough, that very night, an enemy army slipped into the city, killed King Belshazzar, and took over his kingdom. (See: Daniel 5.)

FUN FACTS!
When the Israelites were rebuilding the temple of God, they wouldn't let the Samaritans help them, so the Samaritans built their *own* temple. (See: Ezra 4:1–3; John 4:20.)

Places & People

MAGOG

This northern nation will lead an invasion of Israel someday. Some people believe that Magog is Russia; others say that it's a place in Turkey or somewhere else. (See: Ezekiel 38:1–2; 39:1–2.)

Who's that?

OTHNIEL

A nephew of Caleb from the tribe of Judah. Othniel conquered Debir, a city of giants, in order to marry Caleb's daughter. Othniel later led the Israelites to drive out foreign invaders. (See: Judges 1:11–13; 3:7–11.)

THE NAME GAME!
One Israelite girl from the tribe of Judah was named "Hazzelelponi" (1 Chronicles 4:3). Unfortunately, it *doesn't* mean "a hazel-colored pony." It means "coming shadows."

PAUL

The apostle Paul (first called Saul) started out by persecuting Christians, then had a vision of Jesus and became a Christian. He preached the gospel all over the Roman Empire and wrote half the letters in the New Testament. (See: Acts 8:1–3; 9:1–22; 13:9.)

PETER

Peter (also called Simon) was a fisherman who became one of Jesus' 12 apostles. He was a top leader of the church and performed many miracles. He wrote two letters, 1 Peter and 2 Peter. (See: Matthew 4:18–20; Acts 2:14; 5:12–15.)

STRANGE BUT TRUE!
One time Peter needed some money to pay taxes. So he went fishing, caught a fish, and opened its mouth—and there was a coin in its mouth. (See: Matthew 17:24–27.)

Jesus, walking on the water, rescues Peter—who walked on the water, too, for awhile. The picture is from a church window in Harrisburg, Pennsylvania.

And that Definition Means...

PREACH

In Acts 8:25, the term to *preach the gospel* means to tell or to announce the good news about Jesus. *Preach* also has a special, colorful meaning in Romans 10:8. There *kērussō*, the Greek word for *preach*, means to call out or to proclaim news like a herald of the king. To *preach* can also mean to teach and explain to people how to live godly lives. (See: Romans 2:21; Acts 5:20.)

GOSPEL

Gospel comes from the old Anglo-Saxon word godspell, which means "good news." The gospel is the good news that Jesus has come, that He died to save us and was raised to eternal life. Christians are commanded to preach the gospel. Gospel also means the full story of Jesus' life, all the details that are told in the four Gospels—Matthew, Mark, Luke, and John. (See: Mark 16:15; Romans 1:15–16.)

Feature

WHEN LOCUST ARMIES COME

Locusts are like huge, dark grasshoppers, and a monstrous locust swarm is a terrifying thing. When God was judging Egypt, He sent so many locusts that they made the sky turn dark, covered the entire land so the ground couldn't be seen, and ate everything in sight. It was the worst locust plague in history. But hundreds of years later, the Israelites were disobeying God, so He sent a locust plague on *Israel*! He sent four swarms of locusts—one right after another! They were so destructive and so unstoppable that God compared them to a foreign army invading the land. (See: Exodus 10:4–6, 13–15; Joel 1:1–7; 2:1–11.)

FUN FACTS!

When God sent the plague of locusts on Egypt, they not only covered the entire ground, but they also *filled* the Egyptians' houses. Imagine trying to clean house! (See: Exodus 10:4–6.)

Ten Jobs of Bible Times

1. Farmer
2. Carpenter
3. Potter
4. Barber
5. Scribe or letter writer
6. Fisherman
7. Tax collector
8. Fuller or clothes washer
9. Shepherd
10. Tanner or leather maker

(See: Ruth 2:2–4; 1 Kings 19:19; 2 Chronicles 24:12; Jeremiah 18:1–4; Ezekiel 5:1; 9:2; Matthew 4:18–22; 9:9; 27:7; Mark 6:3; 9:3; Luke 2:8; 19:1–8; Acts 9:43.)

I Love Lists!

Locusts swarming.

PHARAOH

All the kings of Egypt were called Pharaoh. Moses ordered one Pharaoh to let the Israelites go. Hundreds of years later, another Pharaoh named Shishak invaded Israel. (See: Exodus 6:1–13; 1 Kings 14:25–26.)

PHILEMON

A wealthy Christian who lived in Colosse. He was a close friend of the apostle Paul. Paul wrote him a letter asking him to forgive his runaway slave, Onesimus. (See: Philemon 1.)

PHILIP

A deacon of the early church who boldly preached the gospel and performed miracles, and was called "Philip the evangelist" (Acts 21:8 NIV). Years later, Philip had four daughters who were prophetesses. (See: Acts 6:3–5; 8:4–8, 26–40; 21:8–9.)

EVANGELIZE

(See: Preach, page 124, and Witness, page 104.)

GIFTS, SPIRITUAL

Any ability that God's Spirit gives a person as a special gift. In 1 Corinthians 12:1–11, Paul lists some spiritual gifts: wisdom, knowledge, faith, healing, miraculous powers, prophecy, distinguishing between spirits, and speaking in tongues. There are, of course, other spiritual gifts.

TONGUES, GIFT OF

When God poured His Holy Spirit upon the first Christians, they "began to speak with other tongues [foreign languages]" (Acts 2:4 NKJV) that they had never learned. This was a miracle of God. After this, almost every time Christians received the Holy Spirit, they spoke in tongues. Some Christians believe that God still gives the "gift of tongues" today. Others believe that was just for the days of the early church. (See: Acts 2:1–11; 10:44–46.)

Feature

LET'S GET BUILDING!

King Cyrus of Persia gave the Jews permission to rebuild their destroyed temple, but the enemies of the Jews got the next Persian king to stop them. The Jews thought, *Oh well, there's nothing we can do,* so for many years they went about their own business, built their own houses, and left the temple standing half-built. But God sent a drought on their crops, and no matter how hard they worked, they never had enough. The prophet Haggai said that if the people wanted God's blessing, they needed to finish building *His* house first—so they did, and God blessed them. (See: Haggai 1; Ezra 4:1–5:2; 6:13–15.)

STRANGE BUT TRUE!
A lawn on your roof? In Israel, roofs were flat and covered with clay. When it rained, grass sprouted and grew up there. It didn't last long, though. (See: 2 Kings 19:26; Psalm 129:6.)

Four Smelly Situations:

1. The Nile River "stank" (Exodus 7:21 NKJV) when its waters turned to blood.
2. Egypt "reeked" (Exodus 8:14 NIV) with the stench of rotting heaps of frogs.
3. Some manna was "full of maggots and began to smell" (Exodus 16:20 NIV).
4. Martha said that her brother, dead four days, had begun to "stinketh" (John 11:39 KJV).

I Love Lists!

ATHENS

Places & People

Athens was—and still is—an important city of Greece, and was the home of many wise Greek philosophers. The city was also full of statues and idols. Paul preached the gospel there. (See: Acts 17:16–34.)

FUN FACTS!
Sometimes Paul quoted popular poets and playwrights. In a letter to Corinth, he quoted a line from a funny play, *Thais*, written by a Greek named Menander. (See: 1 Corinthians 15:33.)

FUN FACTS!
When Paul spoke on Mars' Hill, he was not standing on a mountain on the planet Mars. He was on the *Areopagus* (Hill of Ares) in Athens, dedicated to the Greek god of war named Ares, who was the same as the Roman God named Mars. (See: Acts 17:19.)

FUN FACTS!
In ancient days, most nations had fancy altars made of bronze or metal for their gods, but God said that His altars should be made of dirt or rough stones. (See: Exodus 20:24–25.)

Ruins of the Acropolis, in modern Athens.

Who's ？ that?

PHINEHAS

A grandson of the high priest, Aaron. Phinehas, a Levite, is famous for killing two sinners—an act that turned away God's wrath and stopped a plague. (See: Exodus 6:25; Numbers 25:1–15.)

PHOEBE

A female servant (deaconess) of the early church. She had helped many people, and when she went to Rome, Paul urged the Romans to give her all the help she needed. (See: Romans 16:1–2.)

PILATE

The weak Roman governor of Judea. Pilate believed that Jesus was innocent and tried to set Him free, but finally gave in to Jesus' enemies and had Him crucified. (See: Matthew 27:11–26.)

FUN FACTS!
If the Israelites ate road kill, they had to bathe, wash their clothes, and be ceremonially unclean until evening. (See: Leviticus 17:15.)

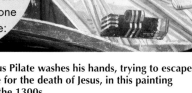

THE NAME GAME!
Gallio was the tough, powerful Roman governor of the city of Corinth, and his word was law. His name, however, wasn't so tough. *Gallio* means "one who lives on milk." (See: Acts 18:12.)

FUN FACTS!
There wasn't just forbidden fruit in Eden. When the Israelites planted fruit trees in Israel, they were forbidden to eat the fruit of it for the first three years. (See: Leviticus 19:23–25.)

Pontius Pilate washes his hands, trying to escape blame for the death of Jesus, in this painting from the 1300s.

And that Definition Means...

CRUCIFIXION

When the Romans wanted to make examples of criminals and rebels, they nailed them to a wooden cross in a public place and let them hang there. Crucifixion was a very slow and painful death: Sometimes the crucified person lasted several hours, sometimes for days. Jesus was crucified on a hill called Golgotha near Jerusalem. (See: Mark 15:22–24.)

DEACON

In the New Testament, a *deacon* was a person who took care of the practical business matters of the church, such as making sure that the poor and widows were fed. Deacons had to be honest and faithful. Most of the deacons of the early church were men, but one lady named Phoebe was a servant of the church—that is, a deaconess. (See: Acts 6:1–6; 1 Timothy 3:8–13; Romans 16:1.)

Feature

DEAD BELIEVERS RETURN TO LIFE AS JESUS DIES!

One of the weirdest stories in the Bible only gets a single, brief mention. When Jesus died on the cross, a lot of other people came back to life. Here's how Matthew described it: "When Jesus had cried out again in a loud voice, he gave up his spirit. At that moment. . .tombs broke open and the bodies of many holy people who had died were raised to life. They came out of the tombs, and after Jesus' resurrection they went into the holy city and appeared to many people" (Matthew 27:50–53 NIV). Why? The Bible doesn't say. But it sure proves how powerful God is!

Places & People

GETHSEMANE, GARDEN OF

Gethsemane was an olive orchard just east of Jerusalem, on the Mount of Olives. Jesus often went there with His disciples to pray. (See: Mark 14:26, 32; Luke 22:39.)

Four Times That Walking Sticks Did Incredible Stuff

1. Moses' staff turned into a snake and later parted the Red Sea.
2. The staffs of Pharaoh's magicians also turned into snakes, which were then swallowed up by Aaron's staff.
3. Aaron's staff blossomed and produced almonds.
4. An angel's staff started a fire.

(See: Exodus 4:2–4; 7:11–12; 14:15–22; Numbers 17:8; Judges 6:21.)

I Love Lists!

The Garden of Gethsemane today.

FUN FACTS!
God said that Israelites couldn't eat blood. He added, "nor may an alien living among you eat blood" (Leviticus 17:12 NIV). These "aliens" weren't Martians. *Alien* simply means "foreigner."

POTIPHAR

Captain of the guard for Pharaoh, king of Egypt. Joseph was his faithful slave, but Potiphar's wife falsely accused him, so Potiphar threw Joseph into prison. (See: Genesis 39.)

FUN FACTS!
When Joseph told his long-lost brothers who he was, he got so emotional and cried so loud that people standing outside his mansion heard him bawling. (See: Genesis 45:1–2.)

PRISCILLA

The wife of Aquila. They were tentmakers and important leaders in the early church. They worked closely with the apostle Paul for many years. (See: Acts 18:1–3, 18–26; Romans 16:3–5.)

PRODIGAL SON

Jesus told a parable about a wealthy man with two sons. The younger son wasted his part of the inheritance but came to his senses, went home to his father, and was forgiven. (See: Luke 15:11–32.)

Loving father forgives foolish son, in a painting from the 1600s.

BODY OF CHRIST

Paul called the Church the Body of Christ. Jesus has His own immortal body, of course, but symbolically He is called the head, and we, the Church—the millions of believers worldwide—are called the body. (See: 1 Corinthians 12:12–27; Ephesians 4:15–16.)

PARABLE

A story that is told to teach a lesson. Jesus' parables were often about common, everyday things—such as a farmer planting grain in his field—but also contained spiritual truths. Jesus told many parables. (See: Matthew 13.)

THE NAME GAME!
Here are two names that only a dad would give his son: *Abinadab,* meaning "my father is generous," and *Abitub,* meaning "my father is good." (See: 1 Samuel 7:1; 1 Chronicles 8:11.)

THE NAME GAME!
Some boys in ancient Israel had the best possible "brother" names: *Ahban* means "brother of intelligence" and *Ahitub* means "brother is good." (See: 1 Chronicles 2:29; 6:11.)

Two oxen wear a wooden yoke.

Seven Famous Farm Tools

1. Sickles—for cutting down grain
2. Ox goads—long sticks to poke oxen and make them move
3. Plows
4. Oxen yokes
5. Axes—for chopping wood
6. Pruning hooks (pruning knives)—for cutting off extra branches
7. Shovels—for tossing grain into the air so wind could blow away the chaff

(See: Deuteronomy 16:9; Judges 3:31; 1 Kings 19:19, 21; 2 Kings 6:4–5; Isaiah 18:5; 30:24; Jeremiah 27:2; Mark 4:29; Luke 9:62.)

I Love Lists!

Feature

JESUS GETS LOST. . .KIND OF

When Jesus was 12, His family went to Jerusalem for the Passover Feast, as they did every year. Jesus walked with the other boys from Nazareth, talking with them. When they headed home, Joseph and Mary thought Jesus was once again with His cousins and friends in the crowd, but when they looked for Him that night, they couldn't find Him! They hurried back to Jerusalem and on the third day found Him in the temple, talking to the teachers of the Law. Whew! God was Jesus' Father, so Jesus told Joseph and Mary that He was there doing His "Father's business" (Luke 2:49 KJV.) (See also: Luke 2:41–51.)

Places & People

CORINTH (CORINTHIANS)

Corinth was a large, wicked city in southern Greece, where Paul met Aquila and Priscilla, preached the gospel for a year and a half, and later wrote two long letters to the churches. (See: Acts 18:1–18.)

Who's that?

RACHEL

Jacob's beautiful second wife. Jacob worked for Rachel's father, Laban, for seven years so he could marry her. Rachel bore Jacob two sons, Joseph and Benjamin. (See: Genesis 29:15–30; 35:24.)

THE NAME GAME!
In the Bible, sometimes even trees were given personal names. Jacob once named a tree *Allon Bacuth*, which means "oak of weeping," marking the spot where Rebekah's nurse was buried. (See: Genesis 35:8.)

RAHAB

A woman living in the city of Jericho who had a bad reputation. Yet Rahab feared God and hid two Israelite spies, so Joshua spared her life when he conquered Jericho. She ended up being an ancestor of Jesus! (See: Joshua 2:1–21; 6:20–25; Matthew 1:5.)

REBEKAH

Sister of Laban, wife of Isaac, and mother of Esau and Jacob. God told Rebekah that Esau would serve his younger brother, Jacob, so she deceived Isaac to make sure that Jacob became heir. (See: Genesis 24; 25:20–26; 27.)

FUN FACTS!
Rebekah was a hard-working young lady! She volunteered to fetch enough jugs full of water for ten camels—and camels can drink a *lot* when they're thirsty. (See: Genesis 24:10, 19–20.)

STRANGE BUT TRUE!
When Esau was born, his whole body was covered with hair like a hairy garment. It's no surprise that they called him *Esau*, which means "hairy." (See: Genesis 25:25.)

And that Definition Means...

ANTICHRIST

John said that "you have heard that the Antichrist is coming" (1 John 2:18 NKJV). Many people believe that the antichrist will appear on earth soon and that he will be a demon-possessed world leader called the beast and the man of sin (the lawless one). He will persecute Christians and demand to be worshipped as God. (See: 2 Thessalonians 2:3–8; Revelation 13.)

SINFUL NATURE

The natural, sinful nature that all people on earth are born with. Paul said, "I know that nothing good lives in me, that is, in my sinful nature" (Romans 7:18 NIV). The King James Version of the Bible calls this the "flesh" (Romans 7:18) or the "old man" (Romans 6:6). It came about as a result of the Fall. When we receive Christ as our Savior, we are set free from having to obey our sinful nature. (See: Romans 7:5–6, 24–25.)

Feature

JESUS SENDS A SWARM OF DEMONS PACKING

One time Jesus crossed the Sea of Galilee and His boat beached near a graveyard. No sooner had He stepped onto land when a berserk, demon-possessed man came rushing out of the tombs. The guy was possessed by a legion of demons. (A

Jesus, wearing a white robe, sends demons from a possessed man into a herd of pigs—which rush over a cliff into the sea. This painting is from 1890.

legion was a group of Roman soldiers, 6,000 men strong!) He was so strong that every time he was bound with iron chains, he snapped them! Now he dropped to his knees and began shouting at the top of his lungs—right in front of Jesus. Jesus commanded, "Come out of the man!" (Mark 5:8 NKJV), and immediately the demons swarmed into a herd of 2,000 pigs. Squealing wildly, the porkers stampeded down a steep slope into the sea and drowned. (See: Mark 5:1–14.)

Places & People

JERICHO

Jericho is an ancient city north of the Dead Sea, near the Jordan River. Its walls fell down in Joshua's day. It was rebuilt, however, and many years later Jesus visited it. (See: Joshua 6:1, 20; Luke 19:1–2.)

Five Verses about Stinking Swine

1. The pig is an "unclean" animal.
2. Boars from the forest lunched on vineyards.
3. A beautiful but foolish woman is like a pig with a gold ring in its snotty snout.
4. Pigs trample priceless pearls in the mud.
5. A freshly washed pig wallows in the mud.

(See: Leviticus 11:7; Psalm 80:8–13; Proverbs 11:22; Matthew 7:6; 2 Peter 2:22.)

I Love Lists!

Nine Times People Hugged, Kissed, and Wept

1. When Jacob met Rachel he kissed her and wept out loud.
2. Esau embraced his long-lost brother Jacob, kissed him, and wept.
3. Joseph wept as he hugged and kissed his 11 brothers.
4–5. Joseph hugged his father twice, weeping and kissing him.
6. Orpah and Ruth wept aloud when Naomi kissed them good-bye.
7. David and Jonathan wept as they kissed each other good-bye.
8. A sinful woman kissed Jesus' feet and washed them with her tears.
9. The elders of Ephesus wept as they kissed and hugged Paul good-bye.

(See: Genesis 29:11; 33:4; 45:14–15; 46:29; 50:1; Ruth 1:4, 8–9; 1 Samuel 20:41; Luke 7:37–38; Acts 20:17–18, 36–38.)

Who's that?

REHOBOAM

Son of Solomon. Because he listened to bad advice, Rehoboam lost the entire northern kingdom (Israel) and was only left with the kingdom of Judah in the south. (See: 1 Kings 12:1–19.)

FUN FACTS!
King Rehoboam was attacked by an angry mob of Israelites, quickly jumped in his chariot, and escaped just in time. (See: 1 Kings 12:18.)

RIZPAH

King Saul's concubine (lesser wife). Saul's son Ishbosheth fought with Abner over her. Rizpah later stood guard over the corpses of her dead sons. (See: 2 Samuel 3:7–12; 21:1–14.)

FUN FACTS!
Back in Old Testament days when guys wanted to insult each other, they said someone was a "dog's head" (like Abner in 2 Samuel 3:8 NIV) or a "dead dog" (like Abishai in 2 Samuel 16:9 NIV).

RUTH

A Moabite woman who loved God. When her husband died, Ruth returned to Israel with her mother-in-law, Naomi, and married Naomi's husband's wealthy cousin Boaz. (See: Ruth 1–4.)

Ruth "gleans," gathering grain dropped by the harvesters, in a field owned by Boaz.

And that Definition Means...

REDEEM, REDEMPTION

To redeem means to buy back something that once belonged to you. For example, Boaz redeemed the field that belonged to his family. Also, we were slaves of sin but Jesus redeemed us. *Agorazō*, which is the Greek word for redeem, means "to buy at the public market." That's where people back then bought slaves. Jesus purchased us with His blood when He died on the cross. (See: Ruth 4:1–9; 1 Peter 1:18–19; Revelation 5:9.)

FUN FACTS!
Ever gone to school and forgotten your lunch at home? Once Jesus' disciples sailed across a lake but forgot to bring bread with them. It happens to us all. (See: Matthew 16:5.)

Feature

WALKING ON WILD, WINDY WAVES

One evening Jesus sent His disciples across the Sea of Galilee in a boat, while He stayed behind and prayed on a hilltop. In the dead of the night the boat was way out at sea, far from land, being tossed around by wind and waves. Already the disciples were worried! But when they saw what they thought was a ghost walking on top of the water, that's when they were completely terrified! They began shouting out in fear, "It is a ghost!" (Matthew 14:26 RSV). But it was just Jesus—walking on top of the wild waves, mind you—and He told them, "It is I; have no fear" (Matthew 14:27 RSV). When He got in the boat, the wind immediately died down. (See: Matthew 14:22–33.)

CAPERNAUM

Places & People

In Jesus' day, Capernaum was a city on the north shore of the Sea of Galilee. Fishermen such as Peter lived there, and Jesus often preached there. (See: Mark 1:21, 29.)

Six of the Richest People in the Bible

1. Abraham was "very wealthy" (Genesis 13:2 NIV).
2. Barzillai was "a very wealthy man" (2 Samuel 19:32 RSV).
3. King Solomon was the richest man on earth.
4. Xerxes, king of Persia, had "vast wealth" (Esther 1:4–7 NIV).
5. Job was the greatest man of the East, and very rich.
6. The rich young ruler had "great possessions" (Matthew 19:22 KJV).

(See: Genesis 24:34–35; 1 Kings 3:13; 10:14–27; Job 1:1–3.)

I Love Lists!

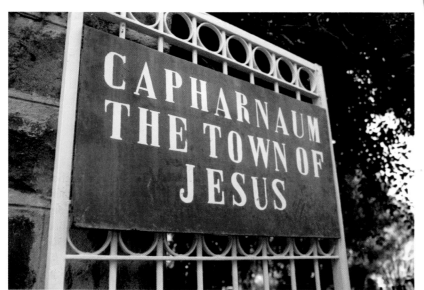

This sign welcomes tourists to modern Capernaum.

Who's
?
that?

SALOME

Daughter of Herodias. The Bible doesn't name her, but historians do. Salome danced for Herod Antipas (her stepfather) then, as a reward, asked for John the Baptist's head on a platter. (See: Matthew 14:3–11.)

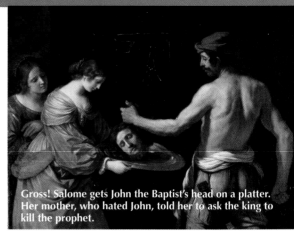

Gross! Salome gets John the Baptist's head on a platter. Her mother, who hated John, told her to ask the king to kill the prophet.

SAMSON

An amazingly strong Israelite who fought the Philistines. The secret of Samson's strength was his long hair. He was betrayed by the Philistine woman Delilah. (See: Judges 13–16.)

FUN FACTS!
Long-haired Samson burned the Philistines' grain-fields, and many years later, long-haired Absalom burned General Joab's grainfield. (See: Judges 15:4–5; 2 Samuel 14:28–30.)

SAMUEL

A great prophet and the last judge of Israel. Samuel anointed Saul as king of Israel, but Saul disobeyed God. Samuel then anointed David as the new king. (See: 1 Samuel 3; 9:27–10:1; 16:1–13.)

And that
Definition ➤
Means...

ANOINT, ANOINTING

To put oil on a person, often by pouring it on his or her head. Oil symbolized the Holy Spirit, and anointing someone set him apart for a special job. Samuel anointed both Saul and David as kings and they became "the Lord's anointed" (1 Samuel 26:9 NKJV). Christians are anointed with the Holy Spirit. (See: 1 Samuel 10:1; 16:13; 2 Corinthians 1:21–22.)

FUN FACTS!
One of the early Christians was named Manaen. He was famous be-cause he was the foster brother of Herod Antipas, wicked ruler of Galilee. As kids they'd grown up together. (See: Acts 13:1.)

FIRSTFRUITS

In Israel, the very first figs and grapes and other fruits to ripen were called *firstfruits*. The Israelites were told to give these firstfruits to God to show that they depended upon Him for the rest of the harvest (Exodus 23:19). It also was a way of showing that they were thankful. Jesus was the "firstfruits" (1 Corinthians 15:20, 23 KJV) of the dead. His resurrection shows that God will also raise all of *us* back to life one day, too. (See: 1 Corinthians 15:20–23.)

Feature

DEAD MAN WALKS OUT OF GRAVE

Jesus had a good friend named Lazarus in the village of Bethany. One day when Jesus was away in Galilee, Lazarus's sisters sent a message saying that Lazarus was very sick. Instead of hurrying there, Jesus stayed two more days in Galilee. By the time He walked all the way to Bethany, Lazarus had been dead for four days, and his sisters and other Jews were mourning him. Jesus had them roll away the stone blocking the tomb, then shouted, "Lazarus, come forth!" (John 11:43 NKJV). To everyone's amazement, the dead man came back to life and walked out of the tomb, wrapped in strips of linen. (See: John 11:1–44.)

FUN FACTS!
The Israelites made a curly "ram's horn" (Exodus 19:13 NIV) into a musical instrument called a *shofar*, and used ram's horns as containers for olive oil to anoint kings. (See: 1 Samuel 16:13.)

Places & People

GAZA

One of the five cities of the Philistines. Samson once visited Gaza and tore the city gates right off their hinges. (See: 1 Samuel 6:17; Judges 16:1–3.)

THE NAME GAME!
Have you heard of the corny cartoon superheroes Heman and Sheerah? They were both named after real-life Bible characters. (See: 1 Chronicles 6:33; 7:24.)

Eight— No, Nine!— Strongman Stunts by Samson

1. Samson tore a lion apart with his bare hands.
2. Samson killed 30 Philistines.
3. Samson attacked the Philistines and killed "many of them" (Judges 15:8 NIV).
4–5. *Twice* Samson ripped apart new ropes that tied him.
6. Samson killed 1,000 Philistines with a donkey's jawbone.
7. Samson ripped off the city gates and left them on top of a hill.
8. Samson ripped seven strong thongs (bowstrings) binding his hands.
9. Samson collapsed a stone temple, killing 3,000 Philistines.

(See: Judges 14:5–6, 19; 15:8, 13–15; 16:3, 6–9, 11–12, 27–30.)

I Love Lists!

SANBALLAT

The godless governor of Samaria in Nehemiah's day. Sanballat constantly tried to stop the Jews from rebuilding Jerusalem's walls. (See: Nehemiah 4:1–2; 6:5–14.)

SARAH

The wife of Abraham. Sarah had no children for many years, but when she was 90, God did a miracle and allowed her to get pregnant and have a son, Isaac. (See: Genesis 17:17; 18:1–15; 21:1–7.)

SATAN

A powerful evil spirit, also called the devil or dragon. Satan rules over demons, hates and accuses good men, leads people astray, and fights God's will. (See: Job 1 – 2; Zechariah 3:1–2; Revelation 12:3, 7–11.)

STRANGE BUT TRUE!
The most bizarre-looking beast in the Bible is a flaming red dragon with seven heads and ten horns. Each of the heads was wearing a crown. (See: Revelation 12:3.)

ASCENSION

After Jesus was raised from the dead, He ascended (went up) to heaven from the Mount of Olives. He was "taken up" from the top of the hill and went straight up until He disappeared in the clouds. This event is called the *ascension*. When Jesus reached heaven, He sat down at the right hand of the throne of God. (See: Mark 16:19; Acts 1:9–12.)

LORD'S DAY

Sunday, the first day of the week, was very important to the early Christians because that was the day that God raised Jesus back to life. Jesus' resurrection was proof that He was the Messiah and Lord, so Christians called Sunday the *Lord's day*. (See: Matthew 28:1–7; Acts 2:32–36; Revelation 1:10.)

The ascension of Jesus, as painted by the classic artist Rembrandt

Feature

JESUS' DEATH-CONQUERING RESURRECTION

Jesus was mercilessly whipped with a cat-o'-nine-tails, then nailed to a cross. Finally, He had a spear thrust through His heart to make sure He was dead. He was then wrapped in linen and buried in a tomb. He lay there dead that day and the whole next day, but early Sunday morning there was a mighty earthquake, and God's Spirit brought Jesus' corpse back to life—and transformed it into a superpowerful body! When some women came to His tomb that morning, Jesus was gone. Only His graveclothes were left. Then Jesus began appearing to His astonished disciples, alive again! Through Jesus' death and resurrection, He rendered Satan powerless against all who are saved! (See: Matthew 27:26–28:10; John 20; Hebrews 2:14.)

FUN FACTS!
In Israel, certain godly, very intelligent women were famous for their advice. Everyone went to them to find out what to do. Each of these ladies was called a "wise woman" (2 Samuel 14:2; 20:16 KJV).

SAMARIA (SAMARITANS)

Places & People

Many non-Jewish foreigners lived in Samaria (central Israel), and the Jews of Judea didn't like them. Jesus, however, showed kindness and love to the Samaritans. (See: John 4:1–42.)

THE NAME GAME!
One Israelite lady had the unusual name of "Hoglah" (Numbers 26:33). It doesn't mean Miss Piggy, though. *Hoglah* actually means "partridge." Wonder if she had a pear tree. . .

Seven Memorable Husband-Wife Conversations

1. Lamech explained to his two wives why he killed someone.
2. Job's wife told her sad, sick husband to "Curse God and die!"
2. Sarah convinced Abraham to take a second wife.
3. Manoah's wife convinced him that he wouldn't die.
4. Samson's wife got him to tell her the answer to his riddle.
5. Jezebel convinced Ahab he deserved to have Naboth's land.
6. The Shunammite woman talked her husband into building a room for Elisha.

(See: Genesis 4:23–24; Job 2:9; Genesis 16:1–3; Judges 13:9–23; 14:1–19; 1 Kings 21:1–16; 2 Kings 4:8–11.)

I Love Lists!

Who's ? that?

SAUL

The first king of Israel. Saul started off humble, but after he repeatedly disobeyed God, the prophet Samuel rebuked him and found a new king. (See: 1 Samuel 10:17–24; 13; 15; 16:1.)

SENNACHERIB

A powerful king of the Assyrian empire. Sennacherib conquered all Judah except for Jerusalem. Because Sennacherib mocked God, God wiped out his huge army. (See: 2 Kings 18:13–19:37.)

SHADRACH

King Nebuchadnezzar threw Shadrach, Meshach, and Abednego into a fiery furnace for refusing to worship his idol, but God protected them. The king then made them officials of Babylon. (See: Daniel 3.)

THE NAME GAME!
One fellow who lived in Israel was named "Gazzam" (Ezra 2:48). If *Gazzam* sounds a bit like *guzzle*, it almost works out to the same thing. It means "consuming."

And that Definition Means...

HELL

Gehenna, the Lake of Fire and Brimstone (the Lake of Burning Sulfur) where the unsaved are punished after they die. It's also called the second death. Some people think there will be actual fire in hell; others think it's symbolic, but whatever hell is, Jesus described it as a place of great suffering. (See: Mark 9:47–48; Revelation 20:11–15; 21:8.)

Shadrach and his two friends— with God's protecting angel— as shown in an English church window.

JUDGMENT SEAT OF CHRIST

God the Father has appointed Jesus to be judge of the world. There will be a separate judgment for the saved when we appear before the judgment seat of Christ. At that time we will be rewarded for the good we have done, and judged for the evil. All of our worthless, unloving deeds will be burned up. (See: Acts 17:31; 1 Corinthians 3:11–15; 2 Corinthians 5:10.)

Feature

PETER DOES ONE MIRACLE AFTER ANOTHER

Peter was the leader of the early church, and one day he met a lame man at the temple gate and commanded him, in Jesus' name, to rise up and walk. The man didn't just walk—he leaped and jumped. After that, Peter became so famous that people brought their sick out into the streets so that as Peter walked by, his shadow might fall on them and heal them. Peter later healed a paralyzed man in Lydda, and the man got up and walked, and when an elderly woman named Tabitha (known as Dorcas to the Greeks) died in the nearby town of Joppa, Peter said, "Tabitha, rise," (Acts 9:40 RSV), and she came back to life and got up. (See: Acts 3:1–10; 5:15; 9:32–42.)

Places & People

MOUNT CARMEL

This mountain is in northern Israel and juts out over the Mediterranean Sea. Elijah called down fire from heaven there to prove that God was the one, true God. (See: 1 Kings 18:19–40.)

Four of the Longest-Lasting Miracles

1. For 40 years the Israelites' clothes didn't wear out and their feet didn't swell.
2. The Israelites had manna every day for 40 years.
3. A pillar of cloud and fire hovered over the Israelite camp 40 years.
4. In Elijah's day, a widow's jars of flour and oil lasted for two or three years.

(See: Deuteronomy 8:4; Exodus 13:20–22; 16:35; 40:36–38; Joshua 5:11–12; 1 Kings 17:14–16; 18:1.)

I love Lists!

THE NAME GAME!

When an Israelite named Nobah conquered the city of Kenath, he decided to rename it. Kenath wouldn't do. "What to call it? Ah, I got it! Let's call it *Nobah!*" (See: Numbers 32:42.)

IMPORTANT IDEA!

Ponce de Leon searched Florida for the Fountain of Youth. There is no Fountain of Youth, but there is a fountain of life. It's with God. (See: Psalm 36:9; Revelation 22:1.)

Who's that?

SHEM

One of Noah's three sons. Shem's brothers were Ham and Japheth. Shem was the ancestor of the Semites, which includes Jews and Arabs and many Asians. (See: Genesis 9:18; 11:10–27.)

SHEMAIAH

A prophet in King Rehoboam's days. He ordered Rehoboam not to go to war against Jeroboam. Shemaiah also caused Rehoboam to repent later. (See: 1 Kings 12:21–24; 2 Chronicles 12:1–12.)

SHIPHRAH

A Hebrew midwife (a woman who delivers babies). Pharaoh ordered Shiphrah and Puah to kill all newborn Hebrew boys, but they disobeyed him. God blessed them for that. (See: Exodus 1:15–21.)

FUN FACTS!
Only two Israelites that we know of were embalmed in Egypt and turned into mummies—Jacob and his son Joseph. (See: Genesis 50:2–3, 26.)

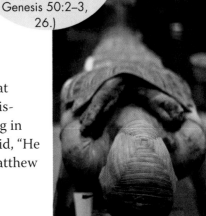

And that Definition Means...

PERSEVERE, PERSEVERANCE

To persevere means to endure, to keep on at something even when it's difficult. For Christians, it means to remain faithful and strong in the faith, no matter what happens. Jesus said, "He who endures to the end shall be saved" (Matthew 24:13 NKJV). (See: Faithfulness, page 154.)

PERSECUTION

When believers are attacked or mocked because of their stand for the truth. Worldly people have persecuted God's people for thousands of years. Jesus was persecuted and promised His disciples that they would be persecuted, too. He advised us to be happy that we were counted worthy to suffer for His sake. (See: Luke 6:22–23; John 15:20; Acts 5:41; Galatians 4:28–29.)

REPENT, REPENTANCE

Peter told people to "Repent, then, and turn to God, so that your sins may be wiped out" (Acts 3:19 NIV). To *repent* doesn't simply mean to feel bad about wrongdoing. It means to stop doing wrong and to literally "have another mind." Paul said we should do things that prove that we have repented. (See: Acts 26:20.)

Feature

SPACED-OUT RHODA

Mark's mother had a large house in Jerusalem, and when Herod Agrippa arrested Peter, many Christians gathered in her house to pray for him. That night, an angel appeared in prison. Peter's chains fell off and the prison doors opened up. Quickly, Peter made his way through the city to Mark's house and knocked on the gate. A girl named Rhoda asked who it was. When Peter said it was he, Rhoda was so overjoyed that she left him standing outside and ran inside with the news. Unfortunately, no one believed her. Meanwhile, Peter was left standing out in the street and, with great perseverance, Peter kept on knocking. . .and knocking. They finally let him in. (See: Acts 12:1–17.)

Places & People

MOUNT OF OLIVES

A long ridge (a hill) just east of Jerusalem. It was covered with olive trees for thousands of years. Jesus rode triumphantly down this mountain into Jerusalem. (See: Mark 11:1–10.)

Six-point Romans Road to Salvation:

1. "For all have sinned" (Romans 3:23 KJV).
2. "The wages of sin is death..." (Romans 6:23 KJV).
3. ". . .But the gift of God is eternal life" (Romans 6:23 KJV).
4. "While we were yet sinners Christ died for us" (Romans 5:8 RSV).
5. " 'Whoever calls on the name of the LORD shall be saved' " (Romans 10:13 NKJV).
6. "If you confess with your mouth, 'Jesus is Lord,' and believe in your heart that God raised him from the dead, you will be saved" (Romans 10:9–10 NIV).

I Love Lists!

The Mount of Olives rises behind the golden Dome of the Rock, a Muslim church, in modern Jerusalem.

THE NAME GAME!
Is God cuddly? An Israelite man named Mishma thought so. He named one of his sons *Hammuel*, which means "God's warmth." (See: 1 Chronicles 4:26.)

SILAS

A Jewish Christian (also called Silvanus) who traveled around the Roman Empire with the apostle Paul, preaching the gospel. Later on, he was a scribe for Peter. (See: Acts 15:40–41; 16 –17; 1 Peter 5:12.)

SIMON THE SORCERER

A Samaritan magician who was called "the Great Power" (Acts 8:10 NIV). Simon sort of believed the gospel but didn't really repent of his evil, power-hungry ways and was cursed. (See: Acts 8:4–25.)

SOLOMON

The son of David and author of three Bible books—Ecclesiastes, Song of Solomon, and most of Proverbs. Solomon was the wisest, richest king Israel ever had. He built a temple for God, but in the end he foolishly began worshipping idols. (See: 1 Kings 3; 4:29–34; 6:1; 11:1–13, 41.)

STRANGE BUT TRUE!
Solomon sent ships to Africa to bring back—among other things—"apes and baboons" (1 Kings 10:22 NIV). He did this every three years. Now, why on earth did he want *so many* baboons?

FUN FACTS!
King Solomon must've had a small army of *hunters* bringing wild meat to his table. Every single day, in addition to beef, Solomon's cooks prepared deer, gazelles, and roebucks. (See: 1 Kings 4:22–23.)

FUN FACTS!
King Solomon had 700 wives. But only one wife—Pharaoh's daughter—was important enough and special enough to get her own palace. (See: 1 Kings 7:8; 11:3; 2 Chronicles 8:11.)

AMBASSADORS OF CHRIST

An ambassador is someone who represents a ruler, or who takes a leader's message to someone else. Paul said that when we witness our faith and urge people to make peace with God, we are acting as "ambassadors for Christ" (2 Corinthians 5:20 KJV).

SANCTIFY, SANCTIFICATION

To be set apart, to be completely given over to God and made holy. Paul said, "For this is the will of God, your sanctification" (1 Thessalonians 4:3 RSV). First Corinthians 6:9–11 gives a clear list of the kinds of unholy people who are not sanctified, compared to those who are. (See Dedicate, page 60.)

Four Wise Sayings (or Proverbs) about Insects

1. Ants have no rulers but store away food for winter.
2. Bloodsucking leeches are greedy.
3. Once again, ants have no one telling them what to do, but do it anyway.
4. Locusts have no king but advance together in ranks.

(See: Proverbs 6:6–8; 30:15, 25, 27.)

Seven Cool Things about the Land of Israel

1. It had springs, pools, and streams.
2. It was full of food—wheat, barley, grapes, figs, pomegranates, and olives. It was " 'a land flowing with milk and honey' " (Deuteronomy 8:8; 11:9 NKJV).
3. The hills were full of copper and iron.
4. God watched over the land all year long.
5. God sent rain in two main rainy seasons—spring and autumn.
6. It was so hot in summer that people took midday siestas.
7. It often rained in one village but not the next village over.

(See: Deuteronomy 8:7, 9; 11:12, 14; 2 Samuel 4:5; Amos 4:7.)

SERGIUS PAULUS AND THE MAGICIAN

Sergius Paulus was the governor of Cyprus, but he was tired of the Roman gods and was looking for spiritual truth. He brought a sorcerer named Elymas into his court, but he still wasn't satisfied. Then one day he heard about Paul and Barnabas and invited them to his palace to preach the gospel. When Elymas argued and tried to turn the governor away from the faith, Paul said, "You son of the devil" (Acts 13:10 NKJV) and commanded, "You shall be blind" (Acts 13:11 NKJV)! At once Elymas became blind and couldn't even see the sun. Sergius Paulus was so amazed that he immediately believed the gospel! (See: Acts 13:4–12.)

Who's that?

STEPHEN

The first Christian martyr. Stephen was a deacon and handled church business matters. He also did miracles and preached the gospel. Religious enemies stoned him to death after he gave a speech that began with the call of Abraham. (See: Acts 6–7.)

TABITHA

A Christian lady of Joppa. Tabitha (also called Dorcas) was a kind woman who often made clothing for others. When she died, Peter came and raised her back to life. (See: Acts 9:36–42.)

TERAH

The father of Abraham. God called Abraham to leave Ur to go to Canaan, but Terah decided the family should stop at Haran and settle down there instead. (See: Genesis 11:27–32; Acts 7:2.)

Stephen sees heaven opened (Acts 7:56) as he's stoned to death for serving Jesus.

THE NAME GAME!
One Bible fellow was named "Pochereth-hazzebaim" (Ezra 2:57 RSV). His name means "gazelle hunter." He'd have liked a New Testament lady named "Tabitha" (Acts 9:36), whose name means "gazelle."

THE NAME GAME!
In ancient Israel, Idbash (1 Chronicles 4:3) was a man's name. Kinda sounds like a guy's name, right?—especially the *bash* part. Actually, *Idbash* means "honey sweet."

THE NAME GAME!
Talk about just being a *number*! Check out these New Testament names. *Secundus* means "second," *Tertius* means "third," and *Quartus* means "fourth." (See Acts 20:4; Romans 16:22–23.)

And that Definition Means...

VISION

Having a vision was like receiving a prophetic dream from God—except that a vision happened when a believer was wide awake, sometimes even with his eyes wide open. Before being stoned, Stephen had a vision of God and Jesus. The apostle Peter once fell into a trance and saw a strange vision of a bed sheet full of animals. Paul had a vision of a man of Macedonia, calling to him to come and help. (See: Acts 7:54–59; 10:9–12; 16:9–10).

Feature

PAUL AND BARNABAS FIGHT AND FORGIVE

Paul and Barnabas were two godly men, and when God told them to go preach the gospel to distant cities, they brought along Barnabas's cousin Mark as their helper. Problem was, Mark deserted them after the first city and headed home. Some months later when they were heading out again, Barnabas wanted to take Mark. Paul disagreed, and he and Barnabas had such a heated argument over it that they parted ways. Fortunately, a few years later Paul and Barnabas were friends again, and Paul even worked together with Mark again. (See: Acts 13:13; 15:36–41; 1 Corinthians 9:6; Colossians 4:10; 2 Timothy 4:11.)

Five Men Who Had Visions of God Sitting on His Throne

1. Isaiah
2. Ezekiel
3. Daniel
4. Stephen
5. John

(See: Isaiah 6:1; Ezekiel 1:26–28; Daniel 7:9–10; Acts 7:55–56; Revelation 4:2–3.)

I Love Lists!

GALATIA (GALATIANS)

Galatia was a Roman province in what is now central Turkey. Paul preached the gospel in many Galatian cities and later wrote a letter to the Galatians. (See: Acts 16:6; Galatians 3:1.)

Places & People

Introduction

The Letter of Paul to the GALATIANS

Who's that?

THOMAS

One of Jesus' 12 apostles. Thomas was very brave and loyal, but when Jesus was raised from the dead, Thomas doubted it. He wanted solid proof before he believed. (See: John 11:7–16; 20:19–29.)

TIMOTHY

One of Paul's closest coworkers. Timothy was Paul's young helper, traveled with him for years, and ended up as the leader of the churches of Ephesus. (See: Acts 16:1–4; 1 Timothy 1:2–3.)

TITUS

One of Paul's fellow workers. Titus was caring and enthusiastic. Paul left him on the island of Crete to teach and organize the churches there. (See: 2 Corinthians 8:16–17; Titus 1:4–5.)

FUN FACTS!
In Jesus' day, Jews often wore *phylacteries*—little boxes with scriptures inside—on their foreheads. Show-offs wore bigger boxes to show how "holy" they were. (See: Matthew 23:5.)

FUN FACTS!
Paul always started his letters with the *same* blessing! Check out Romans 1:7; 1 Corinthians 1:3; 2 Corinthians 1:2; Galatians 1:3; Ephesians 1:2; Philippians 1:2; etc.

A colorful town in modern Crete.

And that Definition Means...

JUSTIFIED, JUSTIFICATION

To be justified means "to be declared free from sin and to be just (righteous)." Jesus lived a perfectly righteous life and died in our place to pay the price for our sins. When we have faith in His sacrifice for us, God justifies us. He looks at us and sees Christ's righteousness. (See: Imputation, page 156; see also: Romans 3:24–25, 28.)

FAITH

(See: Believe, page 96.)

FUN FACTS!
Paul used to persecute and beat Christians, and tried to get them to blaspheme Jesus' name. Then God blinded Paul, and he became a Christian himself! (Acts 8:3; 9:1–19; 26:9–11.)

A statue of Paul in front of an Italian church.

Five Man-Made Laws That Jesus and His Disciples Broke

1. Jesus associated with "unclean" tax collecters and sinners.
2. Jesus' disciples crushed wheat kernels on the Sabbath.
3. Jesus healed people on the Sabbath.
4. Jesus' disciples didn't ceremonially wash up to the elbows before they ate.
5. Jesus' disciples went into the home of "unclean" Gentiles.

(See: Matthew 9:10–12; 11:19; 12:1–6; Mark 3:1–5; 7:1–4; Luke 13:10–16; Acts 10:27–28; 11:2.)

I Love Lists!

Feature

APOSTLE LEFT FOR DEAD

Paul was one of those guys who "took a lickin' and kept on tickin.'" When he and Barnabas healed a lame man in Lystra, the people believed that they were the Greek gods Hermes and Zeus. Paul and Barnabas were barely able to persuade the crowds that they were just men. Then some enemies persuaded the crowds that Paul was an evil villain, so the people—talk about fickle!—dragged him outside the city gates, stoned him with rocks, and left him for dead. But when the Christians gathered around his battered, bleeding body, Paul got up—still alive! He even went back into the city. (See: Acts 14:8–20.)

Places & People

THESSALONICA (THESSALONIANS)

A city in Macedonia (northern Greece). Paul preached the gospel there and later wrote two letters to the persecuted Thessalonian Christians. (See: Acts 17:1–9; 1 Thessalonians 1:1; 2 Thessalonians 1:1.)

Who's that?

TROPHIMUS

A Greek Christian from Ephesus. He traveled with Paul from Greece to Jerusalem, and while there was falsely accused of defiling God's temple. (See: Acts 20:4; 21:27–29.)

FUN FACTS!
Paul was a leader of the Christian church, but since Jesus was a Jew from Nazareth, some Jews called Christians the "sect of the Nazarenes" (Acts 24:5 KJV).

TYRANNUS

A Greek teacher—probably a philosopher—in Ephesus. He let the apostle Paul preach the gospel in his lecture hall for two years, and this really helped spread the gospel. (See: Acts 19:8–10.)

URIAH

One of David's mightiest warriors. Uriah was a Hittite married to Bathsheba, a beautiful Israelite woman, but David had Uriah killed so that he could take his wife. (See: 2 Samuel 11; 23:8, 39.)

STRANGE BUT TRUE!
When Paul was persecuting Christians, God struck him blind. Years later, when Paul was preaching the gospel, he prayed and God struck a bad magician blind. (See: Acts 9:1–9; 13:6–11.)

And that Definition Means...

FEAST OF PENTECOST

This feast was called the Feast of Harvests because it happened at the end of the wheat harvest. It was also called the Feast of Weeks. *Pentecost* means "fifty," and this feast happened seven weeks after Passover, on the fiftieth day. God poured out His Holy

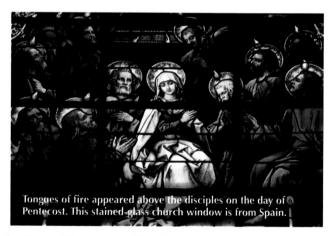

Tongues of fire appeared above the disciples on the day of Pentecost. This stained-glass church window is from Spain.

Spirit on the church on the Day of Pentecost. (See: Deuteronomy 16:9–11; Acts 2:1–4.)

INFILLING (OF HOLY SPIRIT)

To be completely filled with God's Holy Spirit. All Christians receive a measure of the Spirit when they are saved, and being "filled with the Spirit" often happened at the same time. Sometimes this happened a while after they were saved, however. (See: Acts 10:44–45; 19:1–6; Romans 8:9.)

STRANGE BUT TRUE!
God's altar in the temple had metal horns on its four corners, and when people were in trouble they ran in, grabbed hold of two horns, and were safe. (See: Exodus 27:1–2; 1 Kings 1:50–53.)

A British warship on the high seas.

Four Things Agur Simply Couldn't Understand

1. The way of an eagle in the sky
2. The way of a snake on a rock
3. The way of a ship on the high seas
4. The way of a man with a young woman

(See: Proverbs 30:1, 19.)

Five Migrating Birds in the Bible

1. Stork
2. Dove
3. Swift
4. Thrush
5. Quail

(See: Jeremiah 8:7 NIV; Numbers 11:31.)

Six Different Kinds of Owls the Israelites Couldn't Eat

1. Horned owl
2. Screech owl
3. Little owl
4. Great owl
5. White owl
6. Desert owl

(See: Leviticus 11:13, 16–18 NIV)

Feature

IDOLATROUS MOB RIOTS AT EPHESUS

The city of Ephesus worshipped the Roman goddess Diana (Artemis), and they built a magnificent temple for her. The city's silversmiths earned a good living making silver idols to sell. But Paul preached that man-made gods were no gods at all, and many Diana-worshippers became Christians. This angered a silversmith named Demetrius, and he got everyone so stirred up that soon the whole city was in an uproar, screaming how great Diana was. They seized some Christians and dragged them to the amphitheater. No telling what they would have done if a city official hadn't shown up and commanded them to stop rioting. (See: Acts 19.)

Places & People

HITTITES

In Joshua's day, the Hittites were an empire to the north in Turkey. There were also some Hittites (sometimes called sons of Heth) living down south in Canaan. (See: Genesis 23:1–4; Joshua 1:1–4; 9:1–2.)

I Love Lists!

Who's that?

UZZIAH

A king of Judah. For most of his life, Uzziah sought God, and God helped him win many battles. In the end, Uzziah became a leper because of his pride. (See: 2 Chronicles 26.)

VASHTI

The first wife of King Ahaseurus (Xerxes). When the king wanted her to show off her beauty to his nobles, Vashti refused, so he divorced her and picked a new queen Esther. (See: Esther 1; 2:17.)

ZACCHAEUS

A tax collector in Jericho. He was so short he had to climb a tree so that he could see Jesus. After he became a believer, Zacchaeus promised to pay back anyone whom he had cheated. (See: Luke 19:1–10.)

THE NAME GAME!
A Bible character named "Shaashgaz" (Esther 2:14) was the keeper of the Persian king's harem of gorgeous women. Wouldn't you know it?—*Shaashgaz* means "servant of the beautiful."

STRANGE BUT TRUE!
The custom of bells on horses' harnesses (like the kind they wear when pulling sleighs at Christmas) is an old one. Over 2,000 years ago in Israel, horses wore bells, too. (See: Zechariah 14:20.)

STRANGE BUT TRUE!
Elisha had a rare spiritual gift—he could see what was happening in places when he wasn't even there. Jesus had the same ability. (See: 2 Kings 5:19–26; John 1:47–48.)

RESTITUTION

To pay back, to return something that was stolen, or to make good something that was damaged. When Zacchaeus the tax collector repented, he offered to make restitution to (to pay back) any man whom he had cheated. Restitution also means restoring something to the way it originally was. For example, one day God will restore the world to the way it was before the Fall. (See: Luke 19:8; Acts 3:21.)

And that Definition Means...

Paul Revere warns of the approach of the British army.

Six Earth-shaking, Ground-breaking Earthquakes

1. Mount Sinai "trembled violently" (Exodus 19:18 NIV) when God came down.
2. An earthquake shook Mount Horeb when Elijah was there.
3. A devastating earthquake hit in King Uzziah's day.
4. An earthquake struck when Jesus died.
5. A violent earthquake shook Jerusalem at Jesus' resurrection.
6. An earthquake hit Philippi, Greece, and destroyed the local jail where Paul and Silas were imprisoned.

(See: Exodus 19:16–18; 1 Kings 19:8, 11–12; Amos 1:1; Zechariah 14:5; Matthew 27:51, 54; 28:1–2; Acts 16:11–12; 25–26.)

Feature

PAUL'S MIDNIGHT RIDE

Seventeen hundred years before Paul Revere went on his famous midnight ride, another Paul rode a horse for freedom—the apostle Paul. He'd gone to Jerusalem to take money to the poor Christians when he was spotted by his enemies. They went wild and tried to kill Paul, but the Romans rescued him. These enemies then decided to tell the Romans that they wanted to have a "little talk" with Paul the next day—but they planned to ambush and kill him. Fortunately, Paul's nephew heard of the plot and told the Romans, who escorted Paul from Jerusalem at 9:00 that night with 200 soldiers, 70 horsemen, and 200 spearmen. (See: Acts 23:12–33.)

Who's that?

ZADOK

A very godly priest. Abiathar the high priest was disloyal to Solomon, so he lost his job, but because Zadok was loyal, Solomon made him high priest instead. (See: 1 Kings 1:5–8; 2:27, 35.)

ZEBEDEE AND HIS WIFE

A fisherman and the father of James and John. Zebedee's wife traveled to Jerusalem with Jesus and His disciples and made a bold request. (See: Matthew 4:21–22; 20:20–21.)

ZECHARIAH (OF THE OLD TESTAMENT)

A prophet who lived in the days after the Jews returned from Babylon. God's temple had been destroyed, and Zechariah and Haggai encouraged the Jews to rebuild it. (See: Ezra 5:1–2; 6:14.)

FUN FACTS!
King David built a palace in Jerusalem, but about 40 years later King Solomon built a bigger, fancier palace there. No telling what he used the old palace for. (See: 2 Samuel 5:11; 1 Kings 7:1.)

REALLY GROSS!
You never saw a gross plague like *this*! Through Zechariah, God warned that some people's bodies—and their eyes and tongues—would rot while they were standing on their feet! (See: Zechariah 14:12.)

THE NAME GAME!
Zaham was a son of King Rehoboam and Mahalath, David's granddaughter. Some Bible experts say *Zaham* means "fatness." Others think it means "detest." Others say it means "disgusting fool." (See: 2 Chronicles 11:18–19.)

And that Definition Means...

FAITHFUL, FAITHFULNESS

To be reliable and trustworthy. God is faithful in keeping His promises, and that is why we can trust Him. God also calls us to be faithful, to follow Him consistently without giving up, to keep on doing what we're supposed to be

The apostle Paul described people who walked away from their Christian faith as "shipwrecks" (1 Timothy 1:9).

doing. God wants us to "be faithful until death" (Revelation 2:10 NKJV). (See also: Hebrews 10:23; Luke 16:10–12.)

The Pleiades.

Seven Stars, Constellations, and Planets Mentioned in the Scriptures

1–2. Ursa Major *and* Ursa Minor the Bear and its cub
3. Pleiades—the Seven Sisters
4. Orion—the Hunter
5. The star of Bethlehem
6. Saturn—"Chiun" (Amos 5:26 KJV) or "Rephan" (Acts 7:43 NIV)
7. Venus—the Morning Star

(See: Job 9:9; 38:31–32; Amos 5:8, 26; Matthew 2:1–2, 9; Revelation 22:16.)

Six People Who Fled to Egypt for Safety

1. Hadad the Edomite fled from King Solomon.
2. Jeroboam fled from King Solomon.
3. The prophet Uriah fled from King Jehoiakim.
4–6. Joseph, Mary, and Jesus fled from King Herod.

(See: 1 Kings 11:14–19, 40; Jeremiah 26:20–21; Matthew 2:13–14.)

Feature

SAVAGE STORM AND SHIPWRECK

When Paul was sent as a prisoner to Rome, the soldiers booked passage on an Egyptian ship and set out. They were just south of Crete when a terrific hurricane struck and blew them off course. The storm raged for two weeks. For many days and nights, the clouds were so dark they couldn't see either the sun or the stars by which they navigated their ship. Everyone gave up hope of surviving. They were so sick that they stopped eating. Then the ship smashed into some rocks and began breaking apart in the fierce waves. By a miracle, everyone survived: They either swam to shore or hung on to pieces of wood. (See: Acts 27.)

Who's that?

ZECHARIAH (OF THE NEW TESTAMENT)

A priest and the father of John the Baptist. Zechariah saw the angel Gabriel in the temple but doubted his promise, so he was struck speechless for nine months. (See: Luke 1:5–25, 57–79.)

ZEDEKIAH

The last king of Judah. Zedekiah was a weak king who gave in to his nobles and imprisoned Jeremiah. The city and temple were destroyed because of his wrong decisions. (See: Jeremiah 38:1–6; 2 Kings 24:17–25:7.)

ZEPHANIAH

A prophet who wrote the book of Zephaniah. He was probably a cousin of the kings of Judah, and prophesied a lot about the royal court and Jerusalem's destruction. (See: Zephaniah 1:1.)

ZIPPORAH

A Midianite woman and the daughter of Jethro, the priest of Midian. Zipporah married Moses and bore him two sons, Gershom and Eliezer. (See: Exodus 2:15–25; 18:1–4.)

THE NAME GAME!
Sheerah was a grandaughter of Joseph, who oversaw the building of three cities—Lower Beth Horon, Upper Beth Horon, and Uzzen Sheerah. She named the last city after herself. (See: Genesis 46:20; 1 Chronicles 7:22–24.)

THE NAME GAME!
One Bible guy obviously had an older sister named Rachel, because his parents named him *Aharhel*, which means "brother of Rachel." Oh, how humbling! (See: 1 Chronicles 4:8.)

THE NAME GAME!
Canaan was such a dry land and wells were so important that people gave names to them. Isaac called his wells Esek, Sitnah, Rehoboth, and Shibah. (See: Genesis 26:20–22, 33.)

A middle eastern woman at an ancient well.

And that Definition Means...

IMPUTE, IMPUTATION

To declare that something legally belongs to someone—to credit it to them. When we accept that Jesus died in our place, God "imputes" Jesus' righteousness to us. God then no longer counts (imputes) our sins against us. (See: Romans 4:6, 22–24; 2 Corinthians 5:19.)

Feature

PRISONER RESCUES THIEF

When Paul was under house arrest in Rome, he had a surprise visitor from a distant city—Onesimus, a slave of Paul's wealthy friend named Philemon. Even though Philemon had treated him well, Onesimus wanted to be free so badly that he stole money from his master, fled the city, and ended up in Rome. When his money ran out, Onesimus showed up at Paul's house. There he became a Christian. Paul sent him back to Philemon with a letter that asked Philemon to forgive Onesimus and not to treat him like a slave anymore, but as a brother in Christ. (See: Philemon 1.)

Seven Famous Shepherds and Shepherdesses

1) Abel, the son of Adam
2) Lot, Abraham's nephew
3) Rachel, Laban's daughter
4) Jacob (Genesis)
5) Zipporah, Jethro's daughter, future wife of Moses
6) Moses
7) David

(See: Genesis 4:2, 4; 13:5; 29:9–10; 31:36–40; Exodus 2:16, 21; 3:1; 1 Samuel 17:34–35.)

Nine Men of God Who Were in Prison

1. Joseph
2. Samson
3. Micaiah
4. Jeremiah
5. Jehoiachin
6. John the Baptist
7. Peter
8–9. Paul and Silas

(See: Genesis 39:20; Judges 16:20–21; 1 Kings 22:26–27; Jeremiah 37:15; 52:31; Mark 6:17; Acts 16:19–24.)

Prisons are places of punishment for people who've done bad things. But sometimes, innocent and godly people end up in prison, too. God has His own good reasons!

KIDS' BIBLE FACTS INDEX

Art Resource/NY: Pages 14 (Scala), 24 (Snark), 72 (Cameraphoto Arte, Venice), 82 (Scala/Ministero per i Beni e le Attività culturali), 94 (DeA Picture Library), 110 (HIP), 112 (Finsiel/Alinari), 116 (Tate, London), 120 (The Metropolitan Museum of Art), 130 (Alinari), 133 (HIP), 146 (National Gallery, London)

Bildarchiv Preussischer Kulturbesitz/Art Resource/NY: Pages 46, 86, 138

Bill Aron: Page 60

Corbis: Pages 9 (Jean Pierre Fizet/Sygma), 22 (Sunset Boulevard), 26 (John Springer Collection), 58 (William Whitehurst), 62 (Hanan Isachar), 74 (Brooklyn Museum), 76 (Sunset Boulevard), 113 (DLILLC), 115 (Louie Psihoyos), 135 (Brooks Kraft), 153 (PoodlesRock)

Erich Lessing/Art Resource/NY: Pages 12, 42, 49, 54, 78. 128

Flickr: Pages 16, 26, 34, 40, 50, 54 (photopolly), 140

Getty Images: Pages 7 (Hulton Archive), 10 (AFP), 19 (Hulton Archive), 29 (Michael Ochs Archives), 32 (FilmMagic), 53 (Michael Ochs Archives), 81 (AFP), 97 (Premium Archive), 151 (Getty Images News)

Google: Page 64

Gustave Dore: Page 52

iStock: Pages 7, 8, 11, 13, 15, 17, 18, 20, 21, 23, 25, 32, 35, 36, 37, 39, 41, 43, 44, 45, 48, 51, 56, 57, 61, 65, 66, 67, 69, 70, 71, 73, 75, 77, 79, 80, 83, 85, 87, 89, 91, 95, 96, 98, 99, 100, 101, 103, 106, 107, 108, 109, 111, 114, 117, 118, 119, 121, 122, 123, 124, 125, 127, 129, 131, 134, 142, 143, 145, 147, 148, 149, 150, 152, 154, 155, 156, 157

Réunion des Musées Nationaux/Art Resource/NY: Pages 92, 104, 136

Wikipedia: Page 38